LAUGH, CRY AND
REMEMBER

The Journal of
a G.I. Lady

For Ben

a comrade!
WWII.

LAUGH, CRY AND
REMEMBER

The Journal of
a G.I. Lady

Enjoy all

By Clarice F. Pollard

Best Wishes

JOURNEYS PRESS ❦ PHOENIX

Clarice Forty and Pollard

Manufactured in the United States of America.

This edition published by Journeys Press, P.O. Box 32354, Phoenix AZ 85064-2354, (602) 957-4955.

Cover Design By Clarice Pollard—Refined by Mark Woodruff

The symbol on the cover and half title page is the goddess Athena, Goddess of War and Victory.

10   9   8   7   6   5   4   3   2   1

LC 91-90262

Publisher's Cataloging in Publication
Pollard, Clarice F.
   Laugh, cry and remember, The journal of a G.I. lady/ by Clarice F. Pollard.
   p. cm.
ISBN 0-9629334-0-6

   1. Women soldiers—United States—History. 2. World War, 1939-1945—Participation, Female—United States. I. Title.

D769.39   940.5315
                                         QBI91-1510

DEDICATION

To my parents.

DEAR READER:

It is understood that training programs, issuance and use of kinds of clothing, means of housing and the general rules and regulations governing the male and female military varied with the stations or circumstances of occupation.

CONTENTS

ILLUSTRATIONS

FOREWORD

With the mixed emotions of Clarice Pollard's separation as "a soldier in the first permanent female army of the United States" fixed freshly in the heart and mind from reading her remembrance of three years in the WACs, my first reaction is unvarnished admiration for the efforts of her sisters in khaki and olive uniforms who took up the cause of the nation's defense. And especially for Ms. Pollard, who transformed her memories into a venue so others can understand the motivation that sustained her and other WACs.

Women were always involved in America's wars, but until World War II, their participation was unofficial. They loaded guns for their men to fire, nursed the fallen, comforted the bereaved, did without their husbands and sons, or inspired loved ones. Even when "permitted" to serve in our nation's great test against the Axis powers in the first half of the 1940s, they were first considered "auxiliary," not "regular" Army, and even then were resented by a portion of the military and by wives and sweethearts of some servicemen. A reading of this remembrance places all that in perspective; there doubtless were all kinds of WACs, but the sum of their service was more than creditable—it was a crucial dimension in our nation's ultimate victory.

Each reader may find what they wish here. For those of the author's generation, reading these pages will trigger memories of an era of total national commitment, the only time our nation experienced near-unanimous agreement on policy and for the most part willingly sacrificed self for the greater good. Those born afterward can find here a bridge to understanding for their parents' or grandparents' time, and why some of them become misty when seeing old photos and faded uniforms, or when they receive a message from a "buddy" long forgotten. Men *and* women may find here an appreciation for those citizen-soldier pioneers who forced a place for women in the national service.

Pollard is an excellent example of that citizen-soldier. When her country went to war, she became an air-raid warden and USO hostess in Brooklyn, at the time thinking that was all a woman could do. Then she became one of the first enrollees in the Woman's Auxiliary Army Corps and accepted a status that was neither "in" nor "out" of the Army. She trained in Georgia and in Nacogdoches, Texas, in Administration school, then served in the Pacific Northwest, New Orleans, Virginia and finally New York state, enthusiastically tackling drafting, office work, recruiting, entertainment, caring for wounded, and above all, boosting everyone's morale. She and her sisters made it into the Army when they got to drop the "Auxiliary" from their title, for they had earned their stripes by service. Then, despite some bittersweet moments because of the loss of friendships upon her discharge at war's end, re-entered civilian life, mission accomplished.

Pollard grew from her life in the military because she embraced its opportunities; for her, the glass was always half full. Youthful, hopeful, wanting to do her part, she endured the culture shock of leaving Brooklyn, living with different people and always without much privacy. Despite obstacles, she found ways to make military life more than bearable; she accepted it for what it was, a necessary means to a goal, and managed to accumulate far more positive than negative memories and relationships.

Clarice Pollard is not merely a polished, professional writer; she is something more than that. She writes with emotion, with total involvement and with an endearing restraint for the old ways of expression long abandoned by those who think that only the explicit communicates. They are wrong. She is able to communicate much about moral values, patriotism and humanity in her own way. Not a prude by any means and full of joy for living, her experiences in the Army obviously provided her with a sense of purpose and accomplishment. I appreciate her sharing these memories with the rest of us.

—**Archie P. McDonald**
Regents' Professor of History
Stephen F. Austin State University
Nacogdoches, Texas

WORDS BEFORE WORDS

I have related in interviews, articles and stories how I, with my companion soldiers of the first permanent women's army, hurdled the participation-limiting barricades initially set for us by the military during the Second World War. Obversely, I have told how those members of the male population who had always responded to us as sharers in their lives promptly accepted our natural status as partners.

Unfortunately, the antipathetic spoke such phrases as "womankind does not belong in uniform, competent or not," or the dictum, "You cannot get involved because war is man's work." Accompanying the latter viewpoints too were accusations of unbecoming behavior in public and the theory that military sectors of the fair sex were enrolled as camp followers for the diversion of the male warriors.

In nearly every instance, the government investigated, and the tales proved to be hearsay accounts with no basis in truth. Unfortunately, these false reports infiltrated the minds of the gullible and hampered recruitment intended to swell the ranks of ladies in service.

In concert with the choruses of slander and the declarations of "men's work," we dealt with the vestiges of Victorianism clung to by many females uninvolved in either the military forces or the home front war activities; for them, a "woman's place" was still "at home."

Generals Eisenhower and Marshall, who championed our cause and said "give us more women," still were not able to smooth our uphill struggle over the blocks placed in our path, but our course was nonetheless clear: we would not send our men away to fight without doing what we could do to help them win—to this thought we were dedicated. If that meant subordinating ourselves to Army rules and regulations set up to govern us, so be it!

One effect of the early distrust was an ever-present consciousness that we WACs must stand straighter and be more exemplary in conduct than the average mortal, and when we eventually did walk shoulder to shoulder with our male counterparts, we stood even taller because of that.

All days for us were labor days. The hours or sorts of jobs were minor considerations for those committed to the success of the undertaking. Occasional impediments were not permitted to disrupt our work or alter our goals. We knew what we had come to do, and we plied our tasks diligently until the end.

Far too occupied in the war to realize our position and influence in what has now evolved into the women's rights movement, we were out front striding onward and upward, and could only appreciate the consequences of our efforts when we later beheld our inheritors forging ahead through the doors we had opened—and to glory in the sight!

THE 'WHO,' 'WHY'
AND 'WHEREFORE'

The "whys" of putting together my narrative must credit my nearest and dearest who urged that the country's history, and my involvement in it, be recorded as a family journal. My husband, Monroe, daughter Avie Kalker, son Alfred, niece Jeanne Phillis—each authors in their own right—encouraged the first notations between the albums of photographs, Army orders, memorabilia, sketches and letters home. Notations grew into jottings, then became scribblings as one thing remembered touched off another. Scribblings became pages placed in order of their occurence. The page numbers increased as the "whos" and "whys" needed to be answered to satisfy each family member's "wherefores"—each one's area of interest—and all the time the unearthing of my dimming memories from their remote resting place . . . .

Pages, handwritten, ponderous and needing order and clarity for printed form, led to Myra Cameron—neighbor, author and friend. Through the days of creative agonies, Myra waved a wand of encouragement that helped bring all to conclusion in a publishable state.

> . . . and all the while, a perpetual spring of murmurings
> sometimes louder, sometimes softer—unceasing...
> a heartening, inspiring, persistent chorus—
> family, friends, fellow WACs, fellow writers. . . .

I am grateful, too, for Mary Westheimer's guidance and know-how in coaxing narrative into style for publication and for her sage advice; to Mary Hawkins, for gentle suggestions and years of experience in print; and to Mark Woodruff, whose refinements and polishing of my suggested cover design coalesced with my own conceptions.

There are many, many more—unnoted and unnamed—in libraries, government offices, various states of the union and in dusty stockpiles who worked with courtesy, patience and enthusiasm to supply answers and confirm facts. I am appreciative and gratified to have had their help. Yes!—I thank them all!

—**Clarice Fortgang Pollard**
Phoenix, Arizona
July 1991

'I WILL BEAR TRUE
FAITH AND ALLEGIANCE...'

What was I doing posing there uncertainly in that stark, cheerless room wrapped in a white bed sheet and clutching a urine specimen in a container?

I, and several other similarly draped women looked quizzically and hesitatingly at one another, until rescued by a lady in the uniform of the Women's Army Auxiliary Corps who directed us to the proper section of the medical department where we completed our physical examinations. We then dressed, were fingerprinted and completed the pages of questions on the enlistment applications for the Corps that had to do with our personal histories and individual preferences. For instance two examples of the latter were: "Do you mind standing in line for food or other services?" I did, but answered "No." "Does it make you uncomfortable to live and move in groups such as under military circumstances?" to which I again answered "No," although I loved my privacy. I replied in the negative because I felt that I could tolerate these conditions provided they were not to be forever.

Afterward, the Army General Classification Test (AGCT) was administered to be used as a guide for job placement and qualification for leadership. Following the lengthy registration process, we were assigned Army serial numbers and escorted back to the reception area where we were asked to stand as a group and raise our right hands and

I raised mine with the other inductees. We then all faced a WAAC officer who led the declaration of loyalty to the United States, which we intoned together:

> "I, Clarice Fortgang, do solemnly swear that I will support and defend the Constitution of the United States against all enemies foreign and domestic; that I will bear true faith and allegiance to the same, and that I will obey the orders of the President of the United States and the orders of the officers appointed over me according to regulations and uniform code of Military Justice. So help me God."

With those words I became Government Property, a "GI" on inactive status who awaited the call to duty and subject to Auxiliary Corps rules and regulations and at that instant a change occurred—I started to feel different. I observed the same thing happening to the other women around me who also still wore the civilian clothes they had arrived in, but who too were metamorphosing into soldiers! It was now late in the day of February 13, 1943 when the enrollment procedures for entrance into the Corps were finally completed at the Army recruiting office on Whitehall Street in downtown Manhattan.

The phrases of the oath I spoke were the culmination of fourteen months of changes that had taken place in the nation, and in my life. Was I going to take part in a war? Now? Today? How could I? Wars were events that happened long ago to "veterans" who talked of "buddies," far places, and the distant past.

Nevertheless, in the bleak atmosphere of the recruiting office in New York, I was sworn into the Women's Army Auxiliary Corps the eve of Valentine's Day and pledged fealty to the cause of the Allies with whom I hoped to work toward the defeat of the primary Axis powers, namely Germany, Italy and Japan.

We who were enlisted that day drew closer; friendships were formed during this important time together, then, before we parted, many of us exchanged names, addresses and telephone numbers since we were now compatriots. Each went home and awaited the call to duty during which time we kept in touch, talked, and speculated until summoned to active status.

The 26th of February, the telegram arrived that ordered me to report to Fort Oglethorpe, Georgia, on the 12th of March 1943, and as I held the message in my hand I faced another radical change in my way of life. What would it be! My contacts with structured living had been in public school and camp. Discipline I had learned at home, where tasks were required to be completed as were those at school—but what about military order, uniformity, routine? I wondered how and if I could make a meaningful difference in the great effort to bring the conflict to a close!

❧

What circumstances and mood surrounded me at the commencement of March 1943, what atmosphere would I leave behind me in the home I shared with my parents, and in what direction was I headed? I was the third child of four, the oldest being my sister Erma, whose husband, Myron, now served in the Navy, next came Leonard, soon to be drafted whose wife was Lucille, then I, and the youngest was Ruth, married to Phil. Mother was a housewife and teacher, Dad, a salesman for importers of fine laces, and we were a close-knit family.

I had been trained in costume design at the high school level, followed by an apprenticeship in the wholesale garment trade and made further use of my talents when I originated items for the home decorating field. Mother and I eventually formed our own business where we created lamps from old china and glass for interior decorators, which process involved the selection of a suitable piece of antique, with conception of a mounting in a style to enhance the object of art, and the whole completed by being electrified.

We sold unique accessories to accompany the lamps and for other facets of house adornment.

❦

When our world was transformed with the Japanese attack at Pearl Harbor, Hawaii, on the morning of December 7, 1941, and the United States declared war on Japan, it became necessary to add Civilian Defense activities to the work of the day, whereon I became an Air Raid Warden in my immediate neighborhood. With my neighbors I patrolled our streets during the nationally ordered after-dark blackouts of cities and in addition, volunteered as a hostess for the United Service Organization (USO) at Fort Hamilton in Brooklyn, New York. A chance remark on the radio led me to search for the camouflage division of the Army which employed artists to design and construct models in miniature for that department. Numerous inquiries as to their location proved fruitless, but did bring me in contact with information about the newly created Women's Auxiliary Army Corps and subsequently led to the idea of enlisting in the WAAC where the Military could reap larger benefits from my efforts than if I chose to remain within the confines of greater New York. In that case there would not be restrictions on my donation to the war effort, and perhaps even an assignment to the camouflage section?

Life was changing the core of my family, for it was a question of when my brother Leonard was going to be called into the Service. Male friends, neighbors and relatives were in the Armed Forces, and dates began to appear more often in uniform. The tempo of urgency picked up each time I said goodbye to intimates and neighbors with disrupted lives while I prayed that my brother would not have to leave his environs as they had, and I felt a compulsion to stand between him and the enemy. For myself, the thought of dictators who condemned the helpless and abolished the privileges of national and self de-

termination was abhorrent to me, therefore I hoped to contribute to an effort that would deliver the enslaved and
keep my world free of the same.

❦

Now that I was on my way to war, what else would I
part company with other than work, family, friends and
Saturday night dates?

I would forsake the full-fashioned silk hosiery with seams
down the back, saucy pillbox hats with nose veils and my
array of hand-sewn gloves. I would say adieu to the an-
kle-strapped shoes, the fur coat and muff, the spring suits
with nipped-in waists and padded shoulders —but not all
of them—because one blue suit with white cotton blouses,
would accompany me to Basic Training.

❦

When the time came to leave, my companions and I gathered at the specified place in Pennsylvania Station in New
York City to start the journey to Fort Oglethorpe, and as
we moved about the platform amidst the luggage, packages,
clothing, friends and family, we were a lively mass of humanity. I was caught up in the excitement like a butterfly
poised on the brink of a cliff, who when she fluttered her
wings, soared netherward and found herself amid the ebul-
lient cluster of ladies who boarded the special vehicle. We
all selected seats and stowed our belongings, the conductors
shouted their warnings, and as the wheels commenced to
turn, we waved to the figures left behind until they faded
from sight. The motorman then picked up speed, the train
settled down to a steady "clackety clack," we made ourselves
at home, drew cards for "one in the upper" or "two in the
lower" and were off to our unknown, uncharted destination.

In this special accommodation, escorted by an Army nurse and WAAC officer, the ride took three days during which time we traveled through Pennsylvania, Ohio, Kentucky and Tennessee. Along the route we saw other trainloads of uniformed male military personnel. We were six cars of not-quite-soldiers in civilian garb who lounged in seats, walked about, played cards on portable tables, wrote letters or listened to radios and conversationally speculated on the immediate future according to rumor or communication from those already in the forces, as we circulated in the midst of our mountains of possessions.

When at last we approached our terminus in Georgia, just across the borderline from Tennessee, our conveyance slowed, whistles blew and we came to a screeching halt within the confines of the Fort—then from every door streamed ladies with parcels and baggage.

༜

From the moment in March of 1943 when my group pulled out of Pennsylvania Station, until that particular hour on the 19th of January 1946, when I was discharged, I was kept busier by the Army of the United States in more kinds of occupations than I ever could have anticipated.

The trip to Fort Oglethorpe was my first excursion beyond the borders of the District of Columbia. I was devoted to stories written by Roark Bradford in *Collier's* magazine, and on the way to Georgia I saw the real thing: red, red soil and a black man behind a mule with his harness slung across his back from shoulder to hip, plowing furrows in the field. All this appealed to a mind thirsty for the experience of travel and fed a curiosity that will persist to the end of my days.

My first letter home was an introduction to the progress

of my war career and my reaction in that extraordinary period:

March 13, 1943

Saturday Morn 9:30

Dear Folks:

After we entered the cars at Penn Station, the sun came out and we started off on a very pleasant trip. We are on a special train—just for us and we are being waited on hand and foot. Traveled west via the entire state of Pennsylvania for six hours but did stop at Harrisburg, where I dropped the USO card, and also bid "hello" and "goodbye" to Pittsburgh.

We went from Pennsylvania to Ohio and stopped at a place called Dennison at about 9:30. We drew cards for berths—one in an upper and two in a lower. I drew an Ace which gave me the upper—by myself, thank God. About my luggage, it is one of the smallest pieces here. Some of the women have valises as large as trunks and the drugs they are carrying has put my drug department to shame. Everybody has either a cold or some other "krenk"[1]— I feel like an Amazon!

We moved through Columbus, Ohio at 10:30 at night and arrived in Cincinnati at about 11:00 where we remained for 4 hours, then continued on for the rest of the night, and when we awoke this morning at 7, found ourselves in Kentucky. We lingered there two hours while we washed, dressed and had our berths closed. My "wattiss" hurts from sitting, but that is only temporary since there won't be much of it later on.

We've passed several other troop trains coming and going, and do expect to travel for another day since we are going slowly and just taking our time.

Harriet Fau and I located each other soon after we boarded, and we've become fast friends. Her

---

1   *From Yiddish-German* krenk *or* krank, *which means sick. Here used as "ailment."*

brother-in-law, who is associated with the same firm as Daddy, suggested that we meet and that was a great idea.

Right now we're waiting our turn to eat because we've one dining car and six coaches of girls—we go in car by car. A WAAC lieutenant is in charge and an Army nurse officer is riding with us.

I slept well—the berth was very comfortable and we have all the comforts of home, including radios, card tables and enough room to put our feet on the opposite seats.

This is the land of new permanents—and feather cuts. Can't mail this until I am in camp because we sent a porter out with our USO cards at Harrisburg, and he was left behind! Just finished breakfast orange juice—oatmeal, bacon and eggs, rolls and coffee.

Love
Clarice

THE FIRST SALUTE

Here we were at the train station in a real military base with a long line of army trucks waiting to whisk us away, and facing us were white painted one- and two-story cantonments as far as the eye could see, with life and movement provided by soldiers who walked singly or in groups through the narrow streets that separated the buildings of this strange new home. We boarded the olive drab conveyances which were our initiation into several years of that mode of bouncing, rocky transportation, and shortly found ourselves at the WAAC compound where we were greeted by the Cadre under the command of Second Officer Winifred Lewis and her aides, Third Officers Stevenson and Nelson.

The terms that prescribed the ranks of these women had been created for the Auxiliary Corps to avoid confusion with those of the Army of the United States, but the titles of "Second" and "Third Officer" proved unwieldy, therefore they were addressed by the more familiar designation of Lieutenant. They informed us the WAAC area was composed of barracks housing the three platoons which made up our company, with additional buildings for Supply Room, Day Room, Mess Hall and offices. After our First Sergeant was introduced to us, my immediate group followed her inside the designated housing to view the interior of our quarters.

What we saw was a long room faced in raw wood, and aligned along its length were rows of double bunk beds with uncovered mattresses. A drab green metal footlocker stood in front of each bunk, with additional ones placed along the far sides of the facility. Lining the walls were closed wooden cupboards, mounted in pairs at shoulder height, serving each two beds. There were windows between these cabinets allowing the outside light to stream across the room.

The berths and closets were quickly assigned, so we talked while we unpacked and introduced ourselves to any-one we had not met on the train or trucks. Linens, blankets and pillows were distributed and stacked on every mattress, clothes hung from rods beneath the wall closets, possessions lay on beds, cupboard shelves and in and out of the metal floor trunks, and baggage stood all about. I wondered si-lently had I left a home where the bedrooms housed mirrored dressing tables, clothes hung on racks behind closet doors and gracefully draped fabrics outlined the win-dows? There was a vague memory of such a place!

Although friends in the Service had cautioned "Don't vol-unteer," all the well-meant warnings went unheeded, when, within an hour of arrival, a member of the Cadre asked, "Who would be willing. . ."! The willing arms shot up, mine among them, and into the palms of our uplifted hands mop handles were deftly placed. At our feet could be heard the clatter of several pails. We were led to the faucets, filled the buckets, poured in the soap powders and began to wash the bare wood floors—and so commenced Basic Training!

ক্ষ

My title and address were now:
    Auxiliary Clarice M. Fortgang
    Company 6 23rd Regiment
    WAAC Fort Oglethorpe, Georgia

In Camp we were told whom to "Ma'am" and whom to "Sir" and to remember to salute the appropriate parties. "Stand at attention," "stand at ease," "fall out," "fall in," and be "dismissed." It was all a self-consciously new world.

Two "Dog Tags," attached to a neck chain were given to each of us with the notice that they always be worn. In raised lettering on the metal were our names, serial numbers, home addresses, religious preferences and blood types—but what was the indented half circle at one end of the oblong identifications? The reply from a knowing lady was that those notches accommodated the nails used to fasten these labels to a coffin. In the newness of becoming a soldier, that particular function of the tag was a sobering thought.

My wardrobe was a "basic" lot of clothes—no pun intended—for I trusted in the Army system. Instructions received before leaving home said to pack lightly since uniform gear would be issued with no promise as to when, with the result that I lived in the navy blue spring suit I had traveled to camp in and the other few garments I carried with me, doing all training in them for four weeks as did every one of my friends. We wore name badges, and even with the lack of distinguishing gear, we were soldiers every inch of the way!

Mornings turned colder, therefore we were given men's three-quarter-length overcoats which extended to the calf on some ladies and to the anklebone on others. They were allocated randomly "catch as catch can." "Size what?" "You're joking, take it or leave it!" whereon we quickly exchanged articles with one another. WAAC hats, in the shape of visored, box-shaped, flat-topped millinery were issued, and laced brown leather oxfords completed the picture. We each now owned three military items: a hat, shoes and a borrowed outergarment, but an immediate problem developed! The coats were donned in the cool of the early morning when our marching, exercises and classes commenced. The program continued without interruption as temperatures also continued—rising—and we were trapped inside: soaked, perspired messes. To add to our discomfiture gas masks were furnished for chemical warfare training, these to be worn slung over one shoulder of the bulky overcoat and fastened around our distended waists. The masks, having been supplied to all, became part of our permanent apparatus meant to be carried from post to post, although in time many of them were discarded by a number of female soldiers. A year and a half later when we were asked to account for our total allotment of clothing and equipment, I could not locate a pair of khaki-hued stockings only to find them in my gas mask case where they had long reposed since being stowed in a hurried moment. The hosiery, when removed from the environs of the rubber mask, cleared the area for a distance of four beds in every direction. Whew!!

Men's fatigues (jump suits) were distributed too when it became obvious that certain exercises and duties could not be carried out in skirts and other "wear weary" civilian clothes while we awaited military attire. Again these objects were in catch as catch can sizes and once more a reshuffling ensued as with the outercoats. What was lost in fit and femininity was restored when the belt was cinched and a waistline showed, even if vaguely, and we were content with such luxury!

Back to Basic!

Potato peeling started immediately and went on for the duration. Even when I subsequently was assigned to special duty and was offered the option of being excused, I took my turn at KP (Kitchen Police), since I felt it fair to share all chores—and wasn't that what we were there for?

If you eat, girl, you peel!

Yes, we developed a great familiarity with potatoes due to the traditional military diet for both male and female trainees, in which all menus emphasized starches. The theory was that they would be worked off every twenty-four hours—they weren't—with the result that constipation became the order of the day!

Our quarters were provided with sinks but no water closet facilities or showers, necessitating a quarter-mile walk or run to the men's part of camp where toilet and shower installations could be used—each the height of luxury if you were billeted without these essentials. At all

army premises a pan of liquid chemical solution was placed
directly before the shower with posted instructions to walk
through the liquid upon entering and leaving, and also to
dry and dust the toes with the talcum provided. These safe-
guards, which were intended to prevent foot infections,
were dispensed with eventually, and I for one never heard
anyone complain of athlete's foot in my barracks.

If it was daylight, we who dressed for these daily duties,
carried our towels and necessities with us, and when done,
donned those clothes again for the return trip; the daring
wore bathrobes after sundown. In the case of the toilets,
we never observed our officers sprinting the distance required of the enlisted personnel, so deduced that they must
have had some accomodations on the premises.

Conveniences were installed in stages. The first equipment on the list was a row of commodes, placed without
separations, just open and in a line. We were really living!—or were we? Here was the utility we had longed
for—but only a fortunate few could "go!" The opening conversation of the day took place at 6 every morning while
several at a time we lined up on the "Johns,"—the opti-
mistic question of concern posed to one another was
"Anything doin' yet?"

In answer to our desperate quest for relief and regularity,
one foresightful enema bag owner, Jean Kritzer, let it be

6 A.M. Anything doin' yet!

known that deliverance could be in sight if we wished to avail ourselves. I declined, so did the others as each day we "hoped." In time we warmed to her generous offer and our resident bag owner eased our distress when we accepted the loan of the pipe which we passed around to our grateful and "udder" (pun) relief. The Johnny story also had another side and this is how a neophyte soldier dealt with it!— or—"Marcia Gross on and off the toilet seat."

The disciplines of the Army were growing on us but as yet Basic Training was still a budding world. Though "Yes, Ma'am" and "No, Ma'am," "Atten-hut"—"At Ease," "Carry On" and saluting were in constant practice, there sometimes came a cropper, regarding the proper occasion and use of these terms. Our privys as related, stood in full view without the luxury of partitions and doors. One evening, while some women were occupied with the business of their toilette, attended to laundry or were ensconced on a commode, someone spied our Commanding Officer, Lieutenant Lewis, as she entered through one of the doors (with which the room was supplied at both ends), and properly called "Atten-hut!"

On one of the toilets reposed Marcia, ever the earnest Private doing her basic utmost. Caught in the newness of it all and uncertain about whether this was an instance for following the commands she had been taught, Marcia hurriedly arose from her comfortable posture on the seat, to stand at attention with her elbow bent into a salute, then in her confusion, still holding the elbow position, sat, rose and reseated herself several more times. Lieutenant Lewis, who observed these efforts, tried to suppress her laughter as she uttered an "At Ease" order which relieved Marcia of her tense decision, she could then settle down into relaxed contentment, while the officer exited through the opposite side. Such an episode provided drollery, and softened the strains of our soldierly routines.

We remained on the Post long enough to enjoy the luxury of wall separations and curtains for the water closets which provided privacy, and in addition, open showers were added. This was a lavish inheritance for the company that was to follow us into these quarters.

I, too, was in the learning stages and aware of the briefing which quoted the rules and regulations about drinking or having liquor in the barracks. Fledgling soldier that I was, the knowledge that I harbored an eighth of a pint of whiskey in a corked medicine bottle weighed heavily on my conscience because our belongings were always open for inspection. Although it was only intended to be a medicinal nip at the onset of a cold or warm comfort in the first hours of menstruation, I conjured up visions of my detection, punishment, embarrassment and disgrace, and hoped to escape notice until the illegal beverage could be smuggled out and discarded. The post no!—the odor might be a giveaway. I went about ill at ease for days lest I be discovered.

At the end of two weeks, an important event occurred— we were issued the passes that permitted us to leave the limits of the camp. This was my grand opportunity to disencumber myself of my guilty burden! After I had slunk nervously past the Military Police, I heaved a sigh of relief and confided to my companion Kay Jack, with whom I shared this first excursion, that I was carrying "liquor" which must be done away with at the earliest opportunity, and it was, when we arrived in the nearest town—Chattanooga, Tennessee.

My first outing with a military pass entitled me to an overview of the town in its shabby wartime cloak so that my impression of the city was a blur of shoddy Main Street stores, dim lights, fried chicken shacks and floods of soldiers, but it did benevolently provide a place of disposal for my illicit store of contraband, and also allowed me to face the world with a redeemed conscience and a lightened heart, for which I was grateful. I am happy to report that my concern for the considered medical emergencies never materialized.

The unending pursuit of mail exchange did not appear to be reassuring for those of us who were in training, nor for the families at a distance, with the result that many hours were spent trying to place telephone calls to them, or actually succeeding in doing so. This form of communication was a whole evening's occupation that required three procedures: obtaining the proper change, standing in line to use a telephone, then waiting for the connection and response from the other end. Did I say "evening's" occupation?—it seemed to take all night in the slowly moving procession of mostly male personnel.

Because the Spartan attitude of living by the book and doing without had eased to a degree, my feminine psyche, coupled with the need for old familiars reasserted itself, which prompted requests for civilian comforts that started from the ground up. My first requisitions were for corn cure to lessen the soldiers' old complaint, shoe trees for the fastidious care of my foot gear, and a travel iron to assist in the effort toward good grooming, and with subsequent calls, after exchanging news and pleasantries with those I had left behind, the conversation invariably turned to "and could you please send me . . . ."

Letters and telephone talk not withstanding—my father paid a visit to the Army post to see for himself! Everyone fussed over him, enlistees and officers alike, inasmuch as he was our only non-military visitor during the time we were in Fort Oglethorpe. His presence was a treat for all members of my company since he represented every parent and everything that meant "home!"

Daddy was popular not simply because he stood for hearth and homestead, but by reason of the fact that he carried with him a generous handful of girdles for distribution. My father traveled through the southeastern areas where he purchased cotton for these items. His firm, which normally imported French laces, had turned to the manufacture of foundation garments of a satisfying quality during the war emergency. The woven elastic figure persuaders were dear to the hearts of ladies who found that such items were scarce in wartime. Earlier volunteers had them issued to them but we did not, and even if we had brought our own, one more "spare tire" was always welcome—so those who fitted the sizes he carried, received the gifts bountiful.

He arrived on Saturday evening, and on Sunday, Lieutenant Lewis invited him to dine with us which happened to be the one and only occasion we were served baked beans—as a main course! It was difficult to convince him that we did not eat beans regularly, that I had not tried to spare his feelings when I denied that fact, and that Daddy's little girl was not living the life of a recruit in World War I!

❧

Following my parent's visit, I was interviewed for Officer Candidate School (OCS) by our Commanding Officer and urged to go, but did not feel that studies were my forte, and since we were accorded the privilege of accepting or not, I refused. At a later date when the idea held greater appeal for me I still did not apply because I was regularly occupied at one absorbing job or another.

What was involved in the work of Basic Training? How was a routine day spent while in this uncommon atmosphere in preparation for wartime service?

A DAY AT THE WAAC RACES

A new awakening literally took place, this one at 6:00 A.M. following the bugle call to Reveille over the loud speakers, sometimes faintly, sometimes less faintly, depending upon which way the wind was blowing over the huge expanse of Fort Oglethorpe. The brass horn was reinforced by the First Sergeant, who, up and dressed, called from the hallway to all and sundry, "Rise and Shine," "Everybody Up!"

This brought bodies rolling and tumbling from the lower bunks, and others from the upper bunks, who steadied themselves on the frames of the lower ones to climb down. Here and there could be heard wails of "Hey, get your foot off my head!" All was a scramble in the rush for Roll Call for which occasion we appeared in any garments that decently covered our bodies when we stepped outside to answer to the attendance check. We pushed our way through the door, lined up in place and stood with eyes open in fixed staring expressions behind eyelids struggling to close while we answered "Here" when our names were called.

When all had been heard from and "All Present and Accounted For" said by the First Sergeant, the Lieutenant in charge directed some remarks to us and read the orders of the day. We were then free to rush indoors, run through our toilette and don adequate clothing (it was civilian garb up to this point) to be presentable at the "chow-line" in the Mess Hall (dining room). At breakfast we could relax briefly but not enough to lose momentum because our whole day was carried through on it.

Back to the barracks and here commenced the daily cleanup! On arrival we learned that there was an "Army Way" about everything. With one lesson in bed-making, i.e., "Place the undersheet at the edge of the foot of the mattress"—"square corners folded hospital style at the head," the reverse style for the top sheet which was to be six inches from the head (measured with a ruler!) and "tuck the blanket and sheet under please." "Tight," was the name of the game, and could a quarter be bounced on the center of the made-up bed? We all tried!

There were also illustrations and instructions to be followed governing the organization of wardrobe; such as how the long and shorter wearing apparel were to be aligned, the order of items in the wall locker, and footlocker protocol with the prescribed location of articles. Shoes were to be neatly arranged under the hung clothes.

Housekeeping tasks assigned to each were done by weekly rotation and followed the military system of cleaning (forget what you did or didn't do at home). There were floors to be washed, not only in our immediate sphere but in the halls, baths, offices, officers' quarters and lounges. When dusting and polishing were done, dressing took place according to what was available in the pre-uniform days of Basic Training. We then lined up in front of our beds while the officers inspected morning cleanup efforts, personal dress, hygiene, and individual sleeping and wardrobe areas. Infractions ("gigs") were noted and were punishable by the allotment of extra duties.

KP, the Army way, was taught immediately and those assignments were promptly listed, in which case the selected women were up and in the Mess Hall before the official awakening of fellow recruits. For the rest, the day began when the bugle sounded. After attendance check, breakfast, cleanup, inspection and flag raising—all were marched away to classrooms or drill fields (and at some posts, firing ranges or combat training) in the charge of that particular Cadre.

We, who came from every corner of the United States,

united in purpose, were of varied shapes, colors, sizes and kinds—and so was our drill sergeant. A sample of instruction for assuming the proper military posture follows:

> "Yuh thumbs is at yuh sides" . . .
> "Yuh feets is pointing out" . . .
> "Yuh eyes is straight ahead" . . .

So began the Physical Training part of the day during which we exercised, ran and marched—"Hup, two, three, four,"—"foh-ward 'arch," "two, three, four"—"to the ree-ah 'arch"—"two, three, four"—"on the Oblike 'arch. . . .!" This was usually followed by classroom education which included regulations on the wearing of the uniform and questions as to when and where to remove the hat. "Keep all buttons buttoned, tie in place and hair above the collar please!" We discussed Military Courtesy and the acquired habit of the salute, and "did one do it indoors?" We learned about protocol and deference to commissioned personnel—but what about male versus female? Should *we* open the door for *him*—or he for us?—"if *he wants to open the door, let* him!"

In addition we studied the Articles of War, the penalty for absence without leave (AWOL), insubordination, mutiny and drinking on duty. We were schooled on Army Organization, Property Responsibility, Map Reading, First Aid and the Allied Cause. Gas Warfare was on the list too for which practice we were protected by our masks while we walked through tents saturated with chemicals that released noxious vapors. The Basic day was interrupted by lunch hour and Mail Call, also uniform fittings and immunizations. Fire drills were not forgotten by way of alarms that sounded at any hour, and when they did we stood at attention outside our quarters two minutes afterward.

All did not end after evening mess or when dark fell either, for we members of the company were sometimes summoned to fall out again, in which case we dragged our tired bodies from the barracks and practiced marching some more while others were employed at working off their "gigs."

One form of penance was to "police" the grounds which were kept free of litter (Army style) whereon those on that detail picked up everything not the color of earth or pavement. In the case of cigarette butts, the papers were peeled off, rolled between the fingers, then tossed into infinity with the tobacco disbursed into the air. If we had racked up more infractions of the rules, it was an occasion to get the windows washed or anything else tidied that morning chores had not taken care of. If fortune smiled, and we were "gigless," we could be designated to a squad for these miscellaneous duties anyway. Any part of the late day not occupied with cleanup or extra drill was "free," in which case we polished our service shoes with saddle soap, wrote letters, polished the shoes, laundered, chatted, polished shoes, or shopped at the PX (Post Exchange) and again polished those shoes to a sparkling luster.

This was a usual day in Basic Training up to the second that Taps sounded over the loudspeaker at 9 P.M.; then conversation and laughter tapered to a whisper while the lights blinked a farewell and the last recruit tiptoed over the bare floor to her cot. A soothing blanket of quiet spread over all the camp until the peep of the next sunrise, when the first notes of Reveille startled us out of our sleep and summoned us to a new dawn.

❧

One forenoon brought the announcement the company was to prepare for its first big parade. This sent vibrations of excitement through the barracks because the show would include a complete array of the troops at Fort Oglethorpe. When the moment arrived, what an assemblage it was! Soldiers, male and female, were lined up in troop formation, North, East, South and West as far as the eye could see. Flags rippled in the breeze and the instruments of the military bands were burnished until they reflected brilliantly in the sunlight of an April day. While we marched to our places, the musicians played in unison or alternately, with snatches heard in contrapuntal beat that made the wafting sounds reverberate from one to the other through the air.

All about the Platoons, Companies, Brigades and Divisions we could hear the shouts of orders being given—"Atten-hut," "At Ease," or "Forward 'Arch!" There were uniforms with bright ribbon and gold braid trim—their insignia and buttons shined to a dazzling gleam. I was deeply affected by the scene, my heart was aflutter and I was so proud to be a part of it I held my head higher and stood straighter—although I was only a speck in the crowd.

We were issued pieces of uniform in dribs and drabs and participated in the parade dressed in whatever had arrived at Quartermaster in our size. The aim was to have khaki-colored cotton outfits distributed to all, since springtime was in the air and we would be moving out. Procurement of these needs was not easy because there was a war in progress and we of the Women's Army Auxiliary Corps were new in the picture.

ॐ

Halfway through Basic, word came that my brother Leonard had been drafted and would leave home at the end of the next month. This nettled me. I fretted mentally and moaned silently as did my friends during our concentrated efforts to turn ourselves into soldiers to hasten the conclusion of hostilities. I was protective of Leonard in the manner of females since the beginning of time upon their separation from fathers, brothers, husbands, sweethearts and children. They too had wrung their hands and grieved through all the ages of warfare. My brother himself requested no special consideration from me since it had ever been his habit to face the tasks required of him with his complete attention and honest effort. When we volunteers observed the male inductees that poured into the Fort every few days, the picture tore at our heartstrings. We discussed among ourselves our misery at their plight which strengthened the determination to push on—and drive ahead we did!

In the course of this bustling period, letters arrived from friends and relatives, who ignorant of our industrious routine wanted detailed accounts of all activities to satisfy their curiosity, and any recruit was hard put to keep up with this kind of correspondence. The full days continued, but I eked out time to make a sign for our office that indicated our company and regiment number, which we proudly nailed above the doorway. Members of the three platoons even arranged for a party where the girls impersonated officers and non-commissioned officers. I and several other theatrically inclined enlistees participated.

During the month spent at Fort Oglethorpe, we were summoned several times by the medical department for the previously mentioned immunization shots, or to give blood. It seemed to be once a week, although there were likely more days than seven between visits. The shots debilitated a number who agonized for days with their sore arms while they kept the pace required. These vital procedures were done by both experienced and novice medical assistants, and there were some women for whom every visit remained a harrowing ordeal. Most of our programs took place in alphabetical order from Roll Call in the morning to appearances at the clinic for the blood contributions. A friend, whose name preceded mine, invariably fainted at the sight of the needle each time the fluid was drawn. I always escorted her out and admired her courage since she never refused to go, for we were well aware that some soldier at the fighting front would benefit from our donations. We were kept busy, busy, busy—and finally the end of the course was in sight.

❦

"Hot Dawg!" A few days before graduation it was announced that enough summer khakis had arrived to outfit all in proper military uniforms to take to our next stations. These were dress or Class A attire as opposed to other categories of apparel such as work, bed or undergarments, and all such supplies were dispensed through the Quartermaster Department where we were sent in groups. The assortment was arrayed in an area as large as the Waldorf Astoria Hotel ballroom with mountains of male and female clothing spread on tables and hung from racks.

We tried on numerous hats, skirts and other gear until we found ones that fitted us because manufacturers under contract to the Army made them with variations. This was occasioned by the fact that although each maker was supplied with identical patterns, by the time they were cut, sewn, and delivered, the objects had the manufacturer's personal interpretation, which gave each like item an unlike shape and look. An episode related to an article of uniform, the jacket (in Army parlance, the blouse), illustrates the point of the above mentioned diversity as to size and fit: On nearing the area, I groaned at the sight of my friends' acceptance of ill-fitted ones and when it came to my turn, I rejected several offered me by the Sergeant in charge, whereon the conversation took on a different tone while this soldier started to "sell" one to me. The dialogue ensued along the following lines. "This jacket fits you fine, really not too bad," (it was baggy). "You don't like it? Try this one on—you'll love it" (a bigger bag)—"No? Oh, I see you know a well-tailored garment when you see one. Look, don't take what I have here today. I'm gonna have a 'good' outfit for you. Come back Thursday! I'm expecting another shipment! There'll be something that'll be satisfactory—and if you don't like it—you don't have to take it." I did return on Thursday for that "good" Army blouse and a bonus of a well-fitted skirt which pleased both me and the Sergeant.

The difficulty of apparel resources was brought home to me and my associates by a letter from a friend trained at Fort Des Moines, Iowa, whose company the previous month, was sent to work in the cold weather of the Northeast dressed only in seersucker fatigues and thin sweaters. They were met by a cadre of men who wrapped them in army overcoats.

By the last day in Oglethorpe, we all seemed to have accumulated sufficient outer garments to present a unified look, and enough to get us to our following station—where, we were told, we could request from the Quartermaster Department whatever particulars we were lacking.

᳓

The earliest enlistees received everything from inside out, which included girdles, brassieres and bathrobes, but we of the "second wave" were not issued those forementioned parts of the wardrobe. The official list included the following:

4 pair cotton hosiery
4 pair rayon hosiery
2 pair winter pajamas, light blue and white check cotton flannel
2 pair summer pajamas, blue and white striped seersucker
3 slips and 3 panties (beige rayon)
1 olive drab wool jacket
2 olive drab wool skirts
1 winter hat—wool
1 summer hat—beige cotton twill
3 summer cotton twill skirts
1 summer jacket—cotton twill
a fatigue dress, panties, and roller hat of green and white seersucker, and white ankle socks and sneakers.
1 sweater—beige wool
3 cotton shirts
1 tie
2 pair shoes
1 pair galoshes
1 overcoat
1 hooded raincoat

In addition we received:
> a winter overseas (garrison) cap
> a summer overseas (garrison) cap
> leather shoulder purse
> winter gloves—leather
> summer gloves—yellow cotton
> sheer wool off-duty dress
> winter scarf—beige wool
> summer scarf—yellow cotton
> 2 barracks bags

In the case of clothing for special jobs—these too were provided such as: slacks, wool caps, sleeveless sweaters, lumber jackets, etc.

Although we were scheduled by regulation to be supplied with the above pieces of wearables, I had been provided with one pair of shoes, pieces of summer cotton twills with a matching hat, the raincoat and small installments of shirts, hosiery, slips, and panties, all in khaki color. I was given seersucker pajamas because my size was on hand; the rest to be procured (possibly) at the "next place." There was nothing distributed at the "next place," which was Administration School, fortunately located in a warm area—fortunate for the Army and us. Again at the next "next place," the Northwest, the weather was rainy and damp rather than cold, and summer was approaching, for which our wardrobes sufficed.

It was the 15th of April. "Basic" was at an end and now came the time of our first partings. The WAAC had varying requirements for our services, therefore we were prepared as fast as possible while the place of the Corps in the whole picture of the Armed Forces was being ascertained. Dispersed for further education according to needs, and our ratings on the Army General Classification Tests, choices were limited to the following three schools of training: Cooks, Clerks, or Motor Transport.

Everything we now owned we packed in our new barracks bags and in addition, were responsible for any extra accouterments. After a farewell parade, we posed for photographs of one another and also lined up for our first

Army salary which was given to us by a member of the Fiscal Office. This procedure was the same at each location except on the occasion of a furlough, or perhaps an individual change of station when orders and meal tickets accompanied the pay.

My group, scheduled for administrative schooling in Nacogdoches, Texas, was taken to the same station at the Fort whence we had arrived—with our leavetaking detailed in the following letter home.

April 15th, 1943

9:00 a.m.

Dear Folks!

I'm on the train now and the sun is streaming through the windows and we've stopped at a point somewhere near Shreveport, Louisiana. We did board at 2 a.m. in the morning, after having waited from 12 p.m. for the rolling stock to pull in.

Before that we hung around the barracks trying to keep one another awake with beds stripped bare and the whole place looking like the bungalow at Rockaway[1] on the last day of vacation!

At the station, which is right in camp, we stood in the darkness until it grew cold and we raised the hoods of our raincoats. The effect was like the Ku-Klux-Klan ready to start on a night raid. Finally it grew so very cold, the rest of the company went to a nearby schoolhouse to keep warm so two other girls and myself stayed with the luggage to guard it and it was like being back on air raid duty. There wasn't a sound except our own voices. The outlines of our hoods and the luggage in the shadows were reflected eerily by the light of the moon and the stars.

When the train finally arrived, we were lined up and sent in and since our company was last, all the

---

1   *Our family summer cottage at Edgemere, Long Island.*

berths were taken by the time we boarded. All we
had were seats to sit in while half asleep and surrounded by our luggage and packages. At
Chattanooga we were supposed to have a coach attached for us, but it took 2-1/2 hours just to go 9
miles to Chattanooga. Well, at 4:30 a.m. we finally
caught up with the sleeping car and fell into bed. We
arose the next day, (Wednesday) at our leisure and
went in to breakfast. After breakfast we just sat,
read, sang and talked and then had lunch and sat
again.

At Memphis our dining facility was supposed to
be changed, but we didn't arrive until 10:30 at night!

We were allowed to eat eventually, so we went to
the diner and guess how we were served! It was in a
long vehicle about the length of two with connected
tables that were set as necessary, and long benches
on either side of them to sit on just like army
troops—which of course is just what we are! The
sight of that car certainly was unique!

We flopped into bed about 11 and were up at 6:15
this morning.

This train is twice as luxurious as the one we
came down on. Quarters are much larger and more
comfortable (again I have an upper of my own). We
have two dining cars larger than the previous ones
and serving much finer meals.

The scenery since we left camp has been gor-
geous! What beautiful country we have passed. It's
all laid out like the General Motors exhibit at the
World's Fair! Tennessee—(P.S. am just rolling into
Shreveport!) Oh boy! Large buildings—the first
we've seen since New York!

Five minutes later: Some people just gave us a
load of magazines through the windows! At one stop
the USO gave us candy and cigarettes! It's funny
when they do. We did those things for the boys, and
when people do it for us, it feels strange! We forget
that we are in the Army too!

I started to say something about Tennessee; it
has some very clean and well kept country, not
like Pennsylvania or Kentucky which were poor
and filthy! As it was getting dark last night we
came through Louisiana and just missed seeing
the *Mississippi!*

Say I forgot to mention where we're going. It's one of the Army Administration Schools, located in Nacogdoches, Texas, what a name! It's right near Houston, in the eastern central part. We are due in there about 2 this afternoon, but with the way we travel we never know when we'll arrive. We don't move at any set rate of speed, we stop and start, and then stop again to eat when we come to a particularly nice spot.

I always sleep well on the train and well in general. The soil down here is the color of red clay so that the grass and trees and crops are a beautiful color combination! Of course it's spring down here. The colored folks' shacks line some parts of the tracks; they're mostly shabby, dilapidated hovels, and the children come to the doors to watch us pass. The people working in the fields stop and lean on their hoes and shovels to watch us too! The ground is very level and I think it must be low because it isn't too warm yet. We have a window open across the way and it's just nice without jackets.

We must be an awesome sight to a stranger. A carload of WAACs all in beige uniform!

We button ourselves into those shirts and make a very professional looking knot in a very short time. I can get completely dressed in about five minutes-flat, but you won't believe it until you see it! I'll bet!

We're reading, playing cards, talking, visiting, singing and sleeping. Some of the girls have opened the lower seats again and are getting the rest of their sleep.

I think that I've gained about 6 pounds, but I wouldn't like to admit it. I bought a cream to put on my hair after it's washed and it keeps it soft and shiny!

God! Are we ritzy, we have so many porters in attendance! They've seen everything by now since we're all girls and not too formal—of course we're not immodest, just have lots of fun.

We can't mail these letters until we arrive in Nacogdoches—from some of the L.R.'s (Latrine Rumors) we've heard, the school is supposed to be a very fine institution for girls—Stephen F. Austin

College, situated right in town, six ladies to a room and private baths. I wonder what it's really like!

Please don't spread the Administration School notice around too much; I'd like to be successful at it first. It's a six-week course and you know me when it comes to studying.

Only part of the company is here, but mostly my own group, so I think we'll stay together. Those who were selected (?) to go earned the A.F.C.[1] stripe. The girls were split up and sent all over—California, Texas, etc.

I think I'll comb my hair and take a picture on the train. I'm quite suntanned and look pretty dark.

I passed a sign that said "Antiques" on a barn door near Nashville, Tennessee, and I nearly flew out the window!

I'm so absent minded, and Harriet finds everything for me.

We always sing to the tune of "If you knew Suzy"—"she's my upper and I'm her lower, oh! oh! Oh what a team."

One hour later:
Wanted to finish this—but I'm getting ready to pull into port.

Love,
Clarice

---

[1]   *Auxiliary First Class*

THE STUDENT SOLDIER

With 48 states to choose from, the Corps sent some of us to be educated in administrative work on the premises of Stephen F. Austin State Teachers College in Nacogdoches, Texas. Our officers carefully enunciated the name of the town for us: Naah-cuh-dough-chess!

"Port" was the modest train station where we were received by a cadre of WAAC women and army men, all of whom were very snappy looking. One of our girls reflected on the fact that we had trained for a month sans male company then shrieked mockingly for her "Saltpeter Tablets!"

Escorted by the military and a friendly civilian audience of townspeople who seemed happy to have us, we marched in formation through the city to a large white bungalow on the campus which served the purpose of a medical facility. Our baggage followed by truck and was distributed on the ground around us while we lounged about the lawn. I observed that the trees and grass were the intense green color of the artificial ones at the five-and- ten-cent store at home. The red earth, bright flowers and brick college buildings in the distance made a picturesque contrast to the blandness of our late surroundings in Basic Training.

We were invited a few at a time into the clinic, ordered to strip and were examined around our genitals by the nursing staff. The Army was right "up front" about everything except whatever they were looking for. That information they were reluctant to divulge until, with urging, we were informed it was "crabs!" which, up to the moment, I had never heard of.

We were told that members who arrived directly after Basic in wooded areas might be afflicted, which in no way described the bare landscape of Fort Oglethorpe. Precautions, they said, were taken to see that those with the minute lice did not infect the others, but since they detained over half our number, we decided they operated on a quota for each group of arrivals by the You–You–You–and–You method, and chose any number indiscriminately because not one of us complained of itching. We were treated with whatever was calculated to kill the pests, a remedy that smelled of creosote. After this enforced malodorous rest, we prepared to be socially acceptable, were given room assignments and readied ourselves for classes.

The housing at Administration School presented an abrupt change from the two-story barracks we had known to a huge domed building with the outlines of a hay loft. This structure, now to be "home," had been in peacetime the Boys Gym and had lately been divided horizontally allowing for an additional floor to house so many women. Open wall shelving had been installed to hold our smaller belongings, free-standing clothing racks for our uniforms and iron beds to serve our nighttime comfort. The rooms were barn-like in size with one bathroom between each two bedrooms.

There were six women to a room; when four in my dormitory were reassigned, it left me and a friend, Virginia McLaughlin, in spacious luxury, then she was lodged elsewhere and I was alone. On Sundays, I tossed my clothes and accessories helter skelter in careless delight, for on Monday morning the room again had to look strictly GI!

With the glow of a gracious reception, and a view from the campus of graceful homes in plantation style, there was an atmosphere of wealth, spaciousness, and lush greenery. The general look of the town as opposed to Fort Oglethorpe and Chattanooga, suggested that this was a private school for the pampered offspring of oil millionaires. We found that we were not required to do KP, our laundry was taken care of for us, there were civilian cooks and male college students to serve our meals on tin Army trays.

In my initial communication from Nacogdoches to my family I relayed this news, and the fact that after Oglethorpe this was all too rich for my blood!

❦

From the very first, my letters reflected my appreciation for—and innate curiosity about—a world made of humanity from varying environments and locations. People interested me, how they lived, what they thought and occupied themselves with, their effect on me and vice versa.

Now away from home surroundings, I could broaden my experiences, and on that score I was receptive. Conscious of the fact that there was much to be learned about the world, I was eager to absorb whatever would be presented. It was with a full appreciation of the inherent situation, my unique place and uncommon opportunity, that I requested my family keep my letters to them, that I might have an account of my travels, happenings and impressions during this time.

My new title and address were:

Auxiliary First Class Clarice M. Fortgang
Company B. WAAC Branch #1
Army Administration School
Nacogdoches, Texas

❦

The course at Administration School consisted of 52 subjects which required from 1 to 12 hours each of instruction. My nose was going to be to the grindstone since I had neither a photographic mind nor a methodical plodding style. On the other hand, I had a capacity for organization and study that required sitting in solitary concentration. We were cautioned that even with hard work not everyone would make the grade; in that case there were other occupational needs to be filled in the Service.

The teaching staff at Nacogdoches had an assortment of colorful personalities, on campus and in the schoolroom. Their habits of expression were highly individual. For instance, Lieutenant Harrington read all his lessons to us from a notebook which kept him one page ahead of us. With the delivery of a Boy Scout leader giving instructions to an eager troop, he shouted his lessons phrase by phrase as he recited them from his notes, when he misread, he called out "Hold the phone!" or "Wait a minute!"—and recounted the corrected version of the message with one arm raised into the air, index finger pointing at the stars!

In another class, taught by two more of the commissioned personnel, the male officer worked at getting his message across, but according to his alternate, a female who was a stickler for the hard truth, his information was not precise. She would ask politely for time to recite an amendment of the facts, and her meticulous delivery obviously nettled her male colleague who bristled every time she interrupted, which was frequently.

One other feature was a Lieutenant in the WAAC who immediately informed us of her startling credentials. She had graduated from prestigious courses and earned her degrees at a tender age. So that we might not forget what she had accomplished, she regularly reminded us. The intrigue here was a push and pull situation in a romance between her and a male officer who shared the same teaching desk. The object of her affections was a cocky sort, who, in our feminine opinion needed to be brought to heel. With her heart on her sleeve, her tender ego flapped in the wind, and we, ever true to the female view, hoped her cause would triumph in this battle of the vanities.

The interesting members of the cadre continued on to the medical department, whose officer in charge was rarely seen, and anyone on Sick Call was attended to by assistants. Hearsay had it that he was a "party" person who preferred that occupation and the company of agreeable ladies, to the routine requirements of the Army. At a later date when the doctor appeared with an arm in a sling, the rumor was that this gay blade had broken the limb chasing females.

❦

Spring was at hand, Passover and the Easter holidays were in the wings, but no chapel facility was available on the college grounds for the use of any denomination. About town there were churches, but not a synagogue or temple. Happily, arrangements were made for those who wished to observe the anniversary of the exodus of the Jews from Egypt according to their religious custom. I was part of a group invited to a home on Garner, where Lena and Leon Aron had prepared the service and traditional dinner in the form of a buffet.

When young Mr. Aron read the Hebrew passages with his warm Texas drawl, the unaccustomed inflections fell on our Northeastern ears for the first time, and caused hilarity. Each of us eyed the other to see whether the unusual pronunciations were having the same effect—they were. We pressed our lips together to hold back our laughter, until we could no longer stifle our reactions. We communicated our mirth to our host by the expressions on our faces and he and we, all laughed together. We confessed it was the unaccustomed accents, so that our frankness and his responsive wit spread a feeling of closeness and camaraderie about us for the rest of the evening.

Easter came and went in this new atmosphere which meant we were nearing the month of May and approaching us was the famous southwestern heat. For myself and others, our first excursion into 100-degree temperatures made daytime classes an experience to melt the mind. It was a common event to find the prospect of sleep more attractive than the subject at hand, and each hour several students succumbed to the idea only to be shaken awake by a friend or the tenor of the instructor's voice.

Dressed in uniform in this torrid climate, we were permitted to attend instruction without the hat and tie and to unbutton the shirt at the throat while the sleeves remained closed at the wrist. We wore underclothing of brassieres, panties, girdles or garter belts and slips; hosiery and laced oxfords completed our regulation appearance. This was how we looked during any midday in the seasonal warmth. Evenings and Sundays we could either saunter downtown in complete dress with WAAC hats, all buttons buttoned and ties in place or in light civilian cottons, if we had them.

Another first in the process of my education was our presence in tornado country during the course of the hurricane period. On the 10th of May the town buzzed with news that the weather had spawned a storm 20 miles to the northwest of us at noontime in which enormous damage was done to people, homes and property. There had been no sign of untoward weather about the environs of the college which caused us to be thankful to have remained untouched by the calamity.

About this time, I requested from home, items from my personal wardrobe. My reasons were twofold; one, that we were not yet members of the United States Army and were given leave to wear the civilian clothes during off-duty hours about the campus, the other, the extreme heat and my very modest issue of khakis, which allowed few clothing changes. Included were requests for Mother to send me additional brassieres, slips and panties since shopping was difficult and wartime stock limited in quality or choice. I asked too that she scout for pieces of well-tailored summer uniform to add to my wardrobe because "seen as a group, we looked passably good, but individually, we each looked like a sack of wheat with a hat on top."

❦

Events took place at school that I did not write home about. For instance, there was the gastronomical atmosphere. Entering the service meant a new world of living, thinking, dressing, and other unfamiliarities—including varied menus. The expression of these differences became pronounced in the environment of the Administration School dining room.

The service personnel connected with the Mess Hall were civilians hired by the Teachers College under contract with the Women's Army Auxiliary Corps. Local fashions of food preparation were substituted for standard army procedures, that is; vegetables were flavored with bacon, all meats were fried, and eggs were scrambled in lard which were the culinary methods that women from New York, New Jersey, Pennsylvania, and New England were unaccustomed to. Broiling and baking of meats and fresh butter and cream were more familiar to us. Albeit all rations were first class when delivered to every Army installation, the end result varied with the cooks!

When mealtimes became unbearable, a number of us put our heads together and boycotted the dining area. Christine Glovan, Betty Graybecz, others and I bought fruit and milk at a tiny grocery store near the campus and lived on those. We became bloated from our chosen fare, which condition was taken note of by our superiors.

So few of us appeared at Mess times that the officers called a meeting and informed us that prearranged absences were "mutinous" and a subject for punishment if all meals were not attended. We stated our complaints about "fry"—"fry"—"fry." The food continued to be served in grease while we sat dutifully at the tables as commanded. For the remainder of our stay we tolerated this situation and continued to supplement our diet with other purchases! Our food problem occupied a small portion of the day and took its place among routine concerns, and for the rest, we were in Texas to get on with the process of doing what was necessary toward the War effort.

Relaxation was on our schedule too, therefore we took advantage of any free hours and because attendance at the movies was a popular pastime in Nacogdoches, we too visited the local theater. The viewing of *Stagecoach*, the classic motion picture that featured John Wayne and Claire Trevor, was a memorable event. First, it was a Western for which I was a ready-and-steady customer, and second, it was shown in an atmosphere of boot and Stetson wearers and "saddle sitters."

It was not just a movie, but a talking picture both on screen and off, because the audience was audible too and, on occasion, more so than the laconic and thriftily worded cowboys on the screen. The gallery urged the hero on, warned him of impending dangers and hugged the heroine for him if he hesitated.

Comments and criticisms were freely expressed concerning the modes of dress, shapes of hats, types of boots and makes of saddles. In regard to the latter, the biggest guffaw came when members of the audience spotted an English one on a horse in this Western. It all made for hilarious, animated theater and served the purpose of entertainment in a way that the writers, actors, and producers could not have imagined. The story line and drama were secondary to the entertainment provided here and only an all GI audience on a military post shared the like quality of commentary.

Other leisure activities were the farewell show and finishing ceremonies of the previous class of WAACs and the graduation of the civilian students at the State Teachers College. There were baseball games played between our own companies, bathing at Fern Lake, or strolls into town where we talked, shopped and snacked. There was also the pleasure of a morale boost from Brigadier General Don C. Faith, the head of the WAAC Training Command, who came to speak to us, encourage us, love us and know what every one of us was doing there.

For another brief moment, life in Nacogdoches was not only war, uniforms and school. One of our girls, Marcia Gross, had a visitor. Her male friend in the Service provided us with a sense of "grand occasion" and since we were an encampment of nearly all females, we adopted him as our own for the short period of his stay.

Marcia's friend was surrounded and escorted by women from early morning until the end of the day with no hint on his part of any intrusion. He basked in our warmth, and we in his. The consensus was that he had a personality we felt we could fall in love with—all but Marcia—alas, who merely saw him as a friend while he had eyes only for Marcia!

The Business of School

What were we doing on that campus anyway? On any given day we were occupied with the task at hand because the course in Army Administration included 52 subjects as previously mentioned, totaling 176 hours, with study time, military and miscellaneous activities in addition, to be accomplished during a period of 6 weeks. To this end we each applied ourselves according to our talents and the inclination to succeed on our personal levels. Frequent quizzes and cramming were a regular part of the course and our routine, which began on awakening at 6 in the morning.

After breakfast we could pore over the books until 8 o'clock, since the cleanup duties were light. From that hour until 12 noon we were in class, then to lunch and leisure until 1:30, and back at lessons until 5:30 in the evening with Mess at 6. Later we studied or attended to anything we saw fit, such as laundering, ironing, hair washing, showering, shoe polishing, letter writing, shopping or socializing. Some were busy with the details of publishing our school newspaper for which my contribution was caricatures of

our WAAC commander. Still others were drafting plans for
our farewell show.

I had to busy myself industriously to make the grade
since schoolwork had never been my principal road to success, and having done that, I did well on the tests. Each
was approached with caution, principally the one on finan-
cial subjects that included military payrolls. Monies for
change-of-station, travel, overseas service, flight time in the
Air Corps, pay to dependents and longevity of service were
among items to be considered and totaled. How I saw myself
through such challenges is illustrated by the following tale.

I prepared well for this particular examination, sat down
in my assigned seat with confidence, and worked my way
through the questions to number 20 which required the
computed pay of a soldier under various conditions. I
skipped over it with the hope that if I paid no attention
to it, it might blow away, and continued down the list to
the finish.

When I checked my question sheet, I discovered a blank
space and there it was, number 20, big as life and still
unsolved. No gremlin was going to solve it for me—my theory of "2 + 2 = 5" was going to be employed—and I took
the plunge! For a half hour I toiled. I figured this and
added that and was deeply engrossed until I heard a voice
say: "Don't you think it's time to call it quits? You're not
getting paid for overtime."

I looked up and to my embarrassment my eyes met those
of the WAAC officer who spoke those words. She and I were
alone in the room! Everyone had gone while I remained
counting on my fingers and perspiring down to my skin.
I'm happy to say my mark for that day was 89!

ॐ

To give the impression that we, the Army element were
the sole occupants of the College would be to ignore the

very real presence of the non-military students with a class about to be graduated during our tenancy. Since our areas of operation were separate, we rarely saw them. The institution functioned with a skeleton faculty and a small number of pupils, having lost the main contingent to the War.

When we were invited to attend their graduation ceremony, we gathered outside the auditorium as the seniors filed past us in their caps and gowns. On an idyllic sunny afternoon, in a setting of heavily leafed trees that threw patterned shadows on them and their building, the young men and women made for a bittersweet picture. During this difficult period of conflict, they were a modest-sized group, and for these few, a once-in-a-lifetime occasion; the presentation of the degrees they had earned. We members of the WAAC followed them into the assembly room and joined their parents, relations and friends to witness this proud and happy celebration in the midst of our country's turmoil.

In addition to undergraduates of the College and adult residents, there was a third element in town whom we referred to as the "civilian kids"—the boys and girls who after their classes were finished for the day, rode their horses over the grounds in true Western style. They galloped past our classroom windows in the late afternoon when we were still at school. It was my first sight of golden palomino horses, and it seemed that every girl and boy owned one.

The parents of these students and the rest of the townspeople, made a circle of welcome warmth around us and took advantage of every opportunity to show us courtesy and consideration. One way in which they expressed their thoughtfulness was to offer us rides to any place we wished to go. Aware that gas was rationed and accustomed to walking, we were inclined to refuse politely, but we could not do so without hurt feelings all around, with the result that we rode even when walking would have served us very well.

We were as much a curiosity to the folks in the outlying county as they were to us. Farmers, ranchers and their ladies came into town on weekend afternoons from the surrounding areas, the men in their Western best, topped by ten-gallon hats and shod in tooled boots. They stared at us and we stared back. One such related incident was a highlight during our stay in Nacogdoches. This took place on the occasion of the opening of the long-planned USO club on a Saturday evening for which invitations were issued to all WAAC and Army personnel with instructions that we be there at the appointed hour.

How long had it been since we were invited to a party in our honor? We busied ourselves at the scrub and ironing boards, with shampoos and bobby pins; we fussed, primped and perfumed. In my case, I dressed in my good shirt, best skirt and tie and even wore makeup, not my "everyday" face.

Primed, pleased and excited we swept into town and descended on the USO like a khaki horde where we found a crowd of men who had congregated at the entrance. There were some in cowboy clothes, others in denims and straw hats, and all in magnificently polished Western footgear. We excused ourselves and made our way past them. Inside, we and our officers made polite conversation with our hosts and one another beneath the balloons and streamers. The outside spectators filed slowly inside where they surrounded us and stood with their hats in their hands while they stared mutely.

After dignitaries had concluded the opening ceremonies, WAAC and other military officers evaporated into the air, whereon we enlisted personnel who had been ordered to stay, ate the cake, drank the coffee and sipped the punch. In the absence of dancing partners (we weren't being asked) we danced with one another to recorded jitterbug rhythms and love ballads. Following this we decided to entertain the crowd of onlookers and ourselves. WAAC parodies and fun songs provided the inspiration for the choice of numbers—we sang until we had exhausted our repertoire. Alas, our silent audience outlasted us—it then seemed the right time to depart, which we did!

The Old Stone Fort

I first saw it from the distance, in a field away from the college buildings—only the topmost portion showed, the tall grasses nearly obscuring it. What was it? I looked and wondered and planned for the opportunity to satisfy my curiosity.

One day, another girl and I pushed our way through the brush and went to see what it might be. We were fascinated by a structure that appeared to be old and abandoned, made of gigantic stones with rough-hewn doors and windows that were barred with wood. Through some slits we could glimpse pieces of what we guessed were old furnishings.

I visited there several more times, alone and with an interested friend, not realizing, city girls that we were, that insects and snakes abounded. We were fortunate not to meet up with the snakes, but did meet up with the insects! Inquiries netted the following information: the Stone Fort, as it was called, was erected around 1779, was converted to a home in 1828, subsequently to a trading post, courthouse, saloon, church, general store and fort, and in addition had been moved from its original site in town.

As my worldly education continued, I discovered Stephen F. Austin State Teachers College was not a girls' school, but was coeducational. It was in the center of the state near the eastern border and halfway between Dallas in the north and Houston in the south and that the town was not newly settled by far!

My impression of Nacogdoches as a latterday boomtown was amended after my arrival when I learned that buildings just stayed where they were until they crumbled with the passage of time, thus the old Main Street was a part of history that no one considered modernizing. I was educated about living legends and towns that grew out—not up from their beginnings and were not torn down to make way for the new. Thus Nacogdoches showed its age, from the Caddo Indian Mound dating to A.D. 1280, through the early Spanish Mission days of 1716, to the rambling suburban homes of the pre-World War II period.

Nacogdoches citizens had lived under nine flags—the tricolor of France, the flags of Spain and Mexico, the Lone Star, the Confederate flag and the Stars and Stripes were some of the banners that had alternated and waved in the gentle breezes here. The town is the second oldest in Texas and one of the main streets, North Street, the oldest street north of Mexico.

So much for "boomtowns!"

❧

Time flew by. Studying and concerns about grades, marching, strolling through town, baseball games, swimming, socializing and shoe polishing came to an end for us after six weeks when we prepared to finish and move on. Some days previous, rehearsals were added for the WAAC entertainment customarily presented before promotion services. The whole town was invited to both the show and the graduation ritual.

The opening scene of our revue, titled "Unauthorized Abbreviations," was the setting for "The Ladies in White." The curtains parted to reveal a semicircular backdrop with three doors—one marked "Ladies Room," the other two unmarked. Eventually the door to the ladies room opened and a female figure appeared wrapped in a sheet held together with one hand while she carefully balanced a glass jar in the palm of the other. Painted on the jar in large letters was URINE SPECIMEN. She stood a moment, debated with herself silently, then chose an unmarked portal and disappeared through it. At this point the door to the ladies room opened again and another sheeted woman with a specimen timidly crept out, wavered noiselessly, selected another exit and disappeared through it. The pace picked up and doors opened and closed until the stage was flooded with ladies in white. Titters started, then howls of laughter as we recalled ourselves on enlistment day when we did the same things! We received a cup or jar and were told to get a "specimen," which we did—the mystery then was what to do with it after it was procured. We too had faced unmarked doors, had chosen outlets and vanished through them.

This first act in mime was followed by skits and musical numbers that brought voice, dance and more comedy to the remainder of the show. I choreographed the dance movements and designed and made the costumes. I combed the town for supplies, then incorporated fabric and trimmings from all the sources to serve our purposes. Among the finished products were ballet gowns with bodices of blue satin encrusted with silver stars attached to voluminous skirts in broad horizontal stripes of red and white gauze that showed effectively under the theatrical lighting.

After the finale, with applause ringing in our ears, we celebrated, then put studies, exams, rehearsals and show business behind us. True to the view that we were soldiers in wartime, we prepared to be bright-eyed for our graduation exercises the following morning. While we breakfasted and made ready to face the remainder of a busy day, we were complimented in print by the *Daily Sentinel* newspaper, which noted that our revue was more professional than those of the two classes that preceded us.

❦

By 10:15 the next morning, we took our assigned seats in the College auditorium with spectators from the town seated behind us. On the podium sat the Pastor who was to give the invocation, the Commanding Officer of our Administration School and the invited speaker, Colonel Joseph S. Harbison of the Adjutant General's School, Fort Washington, Maryland, as well as assorted enlisted and commissioned WAAC members who would participate in the ceremonies.

During this time of War, services were short and to the point on a day when we had more to do than graduate. At the conclusion we filed out to pose for a class picture. After we were dismissed, we attended to last-minute packing, took snapshots and said our "good-byes." Some of us would be separated and dispersed throughout the United States or out of the country.

Several days prior to finishing the course at the State Teachers College, we were offered a few preferences of station. A friend, Harriet Fau, and I chose the state of Washington. Although I was granted my request, Harriet was ordered to Florida, and therefore I was parted from her and other companions too; Kay Jack and Marcia Gross and many more. Christine Glovan, Betty Graybacz, Gisella Cohn, Ella Dalessandro, Mary Donnelly, Edna Horton, Virginia Laughlin, Anne Shedd and Dorothy Todd were a few of the women who were going to the new post with me.

ॐ

Early the next morning we left Nacogdoches in the same manner we had arrived, by military march to the station with our duffles and other belongings brought separately. We boarded the cars with our mountains of baggage and soon reached our first stop, Dallas, where we could spend the greater part of the day, with orders to be back at the train in the evening. Taken en masse to the Baker Hotel for the midday meal, we caused a furor in the coffee shop because of the difficulty of accommodating so many of us on short notice. After lunch we wandered through the hotel and peeked into a dining room which was elegantly set for a group luncheon. Too late our officers discovered we were to have been feted in that dining room as guests of the hotel management who had been instructed to expect us!

In the jewelry department of Neiman-Marcus, Christine Glovan and I stopped to admire a topaz and diamond bracelet, and in true Texas style, the saleswoman graciously insisted that I slip it on my wrist for the full effect, whereon we mutually admired the extravagant creation. Let me see—at $3,200, I could put down $5, and pay $5 a month for . . . !

Outside the store was a sight occasioned by the War; a lady fare-taker who was employed by the public streetcar system to perform what had traditionally been a man's job. Then we went on to the USO club and there I met two GIs with whom I spent the afternoon strolling about—a warm introduction to that celebrated town.

❦

From Dallas our course took us to Seattle by way of Amarillo, Texas, Denver, Colorado, Cheyenne and Laramie, Wyoming. While on the station platform in Cheyenne, I looked down the main avenue and noticed a handsome man walking in our direction who was a character of a kind seen only in motion pictures. He had a large drooping mustache, legs bowed from riding horses and was attired in colorful cowboy dress, topped by a 10-gallon hat. I alerted my fellow travelers to his presence that all might have a look since he was a novelty for us. We continued on through Boise, Idaho, and Portland, Oregon, where at each stop all dutifully posed for one another's cameras.

At long last we entered the state of Washington and eventually the city of Seattle—the conductors shouted "Last Stop—All Off" which reverberated through the cars as the train chugged to a halt. We stepped out of the coaches, viewed unaccustomed landscapes, looked into strange faces, heard new names and mention of unfamiliar places, one of them—"Fort Lawton". Fort Lawton!—what would we find there!

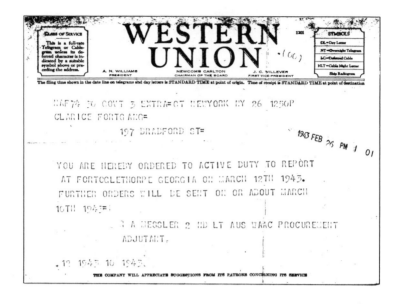

WESTERN UNION

HAF74 30 GOVT 5 EXTRA=GT NEWYORK NY 26 1250P
CLARICE FORTO ANG=
          197 BRADFORD ST=

1943 FEB 26 PM 1 01

YOU ARE HEREBY ORDERED TO ACTIVE DUTY TO REPORT
AT FORTOGLETHORPE GEORGIA ON MARCH 12TH 1943.
FURTHER ORDERS WILL BE SENT ON OR ABOUT MARCH
10TH 1943=

          R A WESSLER 2 ND LT AUS WAAC PROCUREMENT
          ADJUTANT.

.12 1943 10 1943.

Left: Clarice in men's jumpsuit. Right: WAAC hat, WAAC shoes, overcoat and gas mask.

WAAC
SONG-BOOK

Daytona Beach, Florida, February 1943

You WAACs are such a happy crowd
You sing songs old and new,
So now sing long and make it loud
And here's the book for you.

February 1943

Compiled and Edited by

SPECIAL SERVICES BRANCH
SECOND WAAC TRAINING CENTER
Daytona Beach, Florida.

Morning cleanup crew.

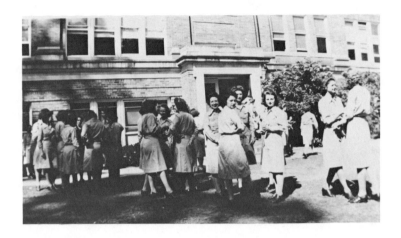

Recess—Stephen F. Austin State College, Nacogdoches, Texas, 1943.

Left: "Lt. Harrington, wait a minute! Hold the phone! April 1943"
Right: Lt. Evelyn Perry caricature, May 1943.

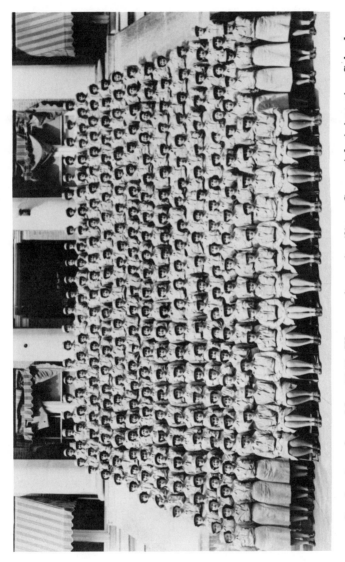

Graduation class, May 1943, Womens Army Auxiliary Corps Administration School in Nacogdoches, Texas.

Today's 60 Cent Luncheon

Hot Chicken Turnover, Creamed Mushroom Sauce

Mashed Potatoes   Macedoine of Vegetables

Banana Meringue Pudding   Bread and Butter

Coffee, Tea or Milk

Chicken Special

80 Cents

OLD FASHION STEWED CHICKEN AND DUMPLINGS

Green Peas   Boiled Potatoes

Bread and Butter   Choice of Sherbets

Coffee, Tea or Milk

TODAY'S SANDWICH SPECIALS ...

Chicken Salad	Salmon Flakes Salad
Mayonnaise On Rye Bread.	On White Bread.
Cole Slaw, Sliced Egg	Sliced Beets,
and Tomato	Cole Slaw
45	35

Baker Special Chef's Salad

with choice of

Crabmeat, Shrimp or Chicken

Served with Our Special Dressing

65 cents

Thursday, May 27, 1943

TODAY'S LUNCHEON [Served from ... 11:30 A. M. to 2 P.M.

Conforming with point rationing, now applying to Hotels and Restaurants.
Please do not request substitutions.

A La Carte ... Old Fashion White Bean Soup 20

COMBINATION SALAD

SPECIAL PLATES

Grilled Supreme of Fresh Gulf Trout, Pimento Butter. 60
Potatoes Familiere. Macedoine of Vegetables.

Diced Ham, Onions, Chives Omelette. 55
Potatoes Familiere. Macedoine of Vegetables.

Fried Filet of Fresh Cod Fish, Tartar Sauce, Cole Slaw. 55
Mashed Potatoes. Buttered New Beets.

Pan Fried Milkfed Veal Cutlet, Paprika Sauce. 65
Mashed Potatoes. Buttered New Beets.

Grilled Pork Chop on Toast, Apple Fritters, Pickled Sauce. 60
Mashed Potatoes. Macedoine of Vegetables.

New England Boiled Dinner, Horseradish Sauce. 60
Potatoes Familiere. Macedoine of Vegetables.

Our Special Fresh Vegetables Luncheon with Creamed Chicken on Toast. 55

Rolls and Butter Served with Hot Plates and Salads

A La Carte ... Roast Prime Ribs of Beef au Jus, Baked Potato .. 110

Desserts ... Vanilla Custard Pie 10   Apple Pie 10   Cherry Pie 10
(Lunch Size) Peach Pie 10   Banana Meringue Pudding 10   Ice Cream or Sherbet 10

Beverages ... Milk, Bottle 10   Buttermilk, Bottle 10   Coffee or Tea 10

Menu, Baker Hotel, Dallas, Texas.

WAAC Administration School graduates from Nacogdoches, Texas, to Seattle, Washington, via Denver.

Clarice and brother Leonard, first furlough.

IN THE GARDEN OF EDEN—
A GOODBYE

On this first day of June 1943, the Evergreen State was
the final destination for our trainload of 138 Women's Army
Auxiliary Corps members; the original 39 that had left Nacogdoches was swelled by more service women who had
boarded the caravan en route. We were separated into two
groups by the WAAC officers whose companies we were to
join. The larger number were Air Forces personnel who
were to be billeted in town, while our smaller segment of
Service Forces, greeted by Third Officer Ida Stoller, was
bound for the Fort. We piled into trucks and started on
our way to our assignment where upon arrival, we joined
a small platoon of ladies from Fort Devens, Massachusetts,
who awaited us to bring their ranks to a full complement.

The humidity and the hills of Seattle slowed us down
for a brief time, but we were granted a few days of leisure
to get our wardrobes in order and sleep in beds that were
not moving on tracks.

The housing and necessities of living we had known in
Basic Training and Administration School had been makeshift and hastily organized due to the fact that we were
a recent addition to the larger picture of the military. By
contrast, our new lodgings, formerly the Bachelor Officers
Quarters, was a long-established storied building surrounded by a lower-level porch with broad central steps
that led to a mahogany door inset with patterned glass.

Inside, polished wood paneling lined the walls of the entrance, the main floor rooms and lounge (Day Room), even the library nook had furniture upholstered in red leather and framed in the same woods. An added advantage was that friends and dates were welcome throughout this whole living room area. Offices, Mess Hall and Officers Quarters completed the first floor.

Our barracks on the upper floors were spacious and airy, and to these rooms we brought a new look as we strolled around in slips, colorful bathrobes, hair in bobby-pins and clips, faces adorned in creams, and manicures in progress. This scene was the order of the day!—none of the men's quarters could boast the same—and "Vive la Différence!"

Now settled in the WAAC zone, we set out to explore the rest of the station. Our senses were dazzled by the Post Theater and an Enlisted Men's Service Club that again had walls rubbed to a rich patina and chairs covered in a bright print to match the draperies. There was a separate dining room where we could purchase a meal, snack, sundae or soda. Another boon was the opportunity to make disc recordings of any messages to be mailed anywhere, so I sent one to my family to their delight and mine.

We were in the Garden of Eden!

In the Post Chapel, there were miniature Bibles made especially for the Armed Forces so I took an Old Testament version and informed my friends, who each took an appropriate one for themselves. What a spiritual lift! I was soon attending Friday evening services, the eve of the Sabbath, which was oftimes companionable because friends of the same and other faiths attended with me where all enjoyed the cake and coffee served afterwards. In the same spirit, we of various persuasions would accompany one another to the Chapel worship on Sunday mornings.

❦

Mail now was to be addressed:
A.F.C. Clarice M. Fortgang
113th WAAC Post Headquarters Company
Fort Lawton, Washington

We were identified as members of the Headquarters Company with passes issued by Lieutenant Stoller, which allowed us on and off the Post. Other means of personal authentication were our dog tags, since they, with all items of clothing and equipment given to us, bore our name and serial number. These evidences of who we were remained constant for all members of the Military and started with the first day of service.

Basic Training was behind us, we were no longer learners at Administration School, now it was time to go to work. Except for those occupied at headquarters, employment was at the Seattle Port of Embarkation outside the Fort, where we became attached to the Army Transportation Corps.

My first placement was in a general administrative job. These typing and office duties lasted three weeks due to the fact that my enlistment record showed my principal occupational listings to be an artist and designer (with office skills secondary) which was referred to as a "rare bird" category. The day these personal skills were noted and I was redeployed to use them, was the turning point in my Army career. I was sent for by the Drafting and Blueprint Section of the Control Department to join the other draftsman there, an architect in civilian life, to make charts and graphs and draw maps that involved the movements of our men and stores in the Western Alaskan and Aleutian Islands regions.

When the latest lists appeared in our office, the two of us had frenetic periods at our drawing tables as our fingers flew over the papers using our pens and slide rulers. We depicted the quantities of soldiers already stationed and their current supplies, and too, the numbers of troops presently embarking with the amounts of food, clothing and war matériel that were to accompany them to their various strategic sites. Like records were drawn on the maps, showing locations of said units with all pertinent information entered up to the minute. We had less frenzied times where we could sit back and relax—but on the alert, awaiting the arrival of new statistics.

There was no training for this work; if one had the hands of an artist coupled with a sense of creativity, those attributes were an asset when a novel method was needed to illustrate whatever necessary. During the periods when my partner or I was on furlough, one or the other did the work of two at a furious pace. With this occupation my geographical horizons were extended while I became familiar with names such as Attu, Kiska, Adak, Atka, Umnak, Unimak and Unalaska, the islands of the Aleutians.

Our drawings were "classified" which in this case meant they were "Secret and Confidential" material; therefore, before I was certified to handle information in this category the Federal Bureau of Investigation delved into my background with personal visits to neighbors at home who had known me since I was a toddler, and they in turn reported to me through my family. In relation to the required proof of one's honesty and patriotism, a memorable incident lingers long in my thoughts.

When the fore-mentioned maps, graphs and charts were finished, they were routinely facsimiled for quick distribution to various interested departments which necessitated taking the original drawings to another building where the duplicating machine was situated. One day, on my return to the drafting section, I discovered a copy was missing! I was the proverbial nervous wreck lest the information contained therein cause an advantage to the enemy whose presence, I thought, lurked behind every pole! Such was not the case—but for a number of days I was less than my confident self.

❦

Although I was grateful to be placed where I could put forth my best efforts, I was aware that not all our women were in that fortunate position because we existed in an atmosphere where we were accepted by some of the men, looked at with curiosity by more, and with the remainder, had to prove ourselves every day for our place in the Military. In the latter classification was the Commander of the Post at Fort Lawton.

At one point when additional administrative help was requisitioned, a platoon of ladies arrived from Motor Transport School by error. Trained, primed and eager to work, they were instead ordered to perform office jobs, but they in turn vowed to toil only for the Motor Corps Division and remained at the barracks each day while the rest of us departed for our duties. Lieutenant Stoller represented them in an arena where "women's place" was not in the Motor Corps and eventually a state of truce was reached when the Post Commander agreed to allow them a trial period at their chosen tasks. They were successful and found recognition as a regular part of his forces.

❦

I was installed at work for some time, had attained a plateau of assurance, the town had become more familiar during the trips to the Port in our Army trucks, and now I was about to go public.

On the occasion of my initial excursion into Seattle from Fort Lawton, I alighted from the bus, stepped off the curb and started briskly across the street without waiting for the proper green light, when a booming voice, magnified by a loud speaker system, addressed me. "The WAAC crossing the street against the light will please take notice that she is not in New York and she is jaywalking!"

Startled and embarrassed, I reached my goal and was immediately approached by the policeman whose voice I had heard. I had made his day! His first female soldier! He good-naturedly reprimanded me and sent me on my way!

I made myself further at home in the city by doing my usual curiosity seeking on and off the main streets which lent color and interest to my days. One notable discovery was a store that dealt in unclaimed freight that was a treasury of varied surprises. There I found my favorite face creams and makeup oddments. An avid tea drinker, I unearthed in their shipment of imported foods, teas from around the world and honey of every flavor. I soon had an exotic little store cached in my closet.

My arrival in Fort Lawton held a more affectionate attraction for me than just the place where I was to be posted. When that part of the military machine responsible for such functions responded to my request for location in Seattle, it also placed me within reasonable contact with a close friend, a medical officer stationed at Fort Lewis in Tacoma.

Captain Irving Reiff and I were able to see one another when convenient which circumstance did not come about easily owing to a question of clarity regarding the rules of fraternization between enlisted and commissioned personnel. Lieutenant Stoller, anxious to further an obviously romantic liaison, offered her quarters for a "tête-a-tête" which we took advantage of, but as time went by we went around town together unselfconsciously due to the fact that the regulations on the matter remained unclear.

In June of 1943 and for the duration of the War my concerns were not only about my immediate person; I carried on an extensive correspondence which was attended to when time allowed. Priorities, in addition to my current sweetheart, were Mother and Dad, sisters Erma and Ruth, those in the Armed Forces; such as my brother Leonard, Erma's husband Myron, cousins Dick and Bill, and Mother's youngest brother, Uncle Mack, and other men I knew in the Services; second considerations were interested friends, neighbors and a fringe of acquaintances. No-mail was a slow day, much mail was a happy bonanza, but also meant replies for which there was sometimes limited opportunity.

From my family's communications to me this month of June, I noted happily that Dad had made his way to Fort Eustis, Virginia, to visit Leonard in Basic Training just as he had come to see me in Fort Oglethorpe.

In my letters home, I bombarded them with questions about the well-being of the aforementioned uniformed members of the family in distant places, and had they any news that I had not? I described the WAAC routine, for I realized our special place in the scheme of our country's efforts and I requested Mother to send particulars regarding sales of our antique stock, which business we conducted together, and guided her attempts at restoration of these items. I cautioned everyone about writing or saying anything regarding our work or location that might be revealing and give aid to the enemy! I wrote that I felt a sense of Old Home Week when I met more servicemen from Brooklyn, mentioned I had dated several, and that spending time with any fellow at Fort Lawton consisted of a walking tour of the Post. I noted that when I had my first appointment off the Base, my escort and I ate dinner followed by a movie, of which we saw only half, in order to return for bed check at our respective barracks. (Seeing part of a show was a procedure that was to be repeated regularly afterward.)

I also reported that the United Service Organizations opened a Club for us in town that was grand, but the pens provided at the writing desks were in the same debilitated state of those in banks and post offices—while I scratched my way through that particular letter!

❧

A group of colored soldiers who worked at the Port practiced and performed fancy drill on the docks at lunch hour. They did their "hup, two-three-fours" to a jazzy beat which provided a great show and were vocal too as they spoke out and counted their numbers in perfect rhythm and harmony. Whether they inspired our Commanding Officer or not, I don't know, except that we too formed a team of which I became a member. We were a platoon of 24 girls who were selected for the purpose of performing before games or between innings at the baseball park and other public events. It was exhilarating and fun since our exercises were done to jazz rhythms like those of the men at the docks.

In the course of time there was more serious marching to be done and a reminder of the whys and wherefores of what the WAAC and other forces were doing in Seattle and around the globe. On the Fourth of July, 1943, my detachment participated in our first public parade for which occasion we were reviewed by the Secretary of the Navy, Frank Knox. All had been practice until then when we hit the Big Time.

We assembled on Third Avenue joined by the other Armed Forces, male and female, and accompanied by Ground, Air and Naval hardware, so that we, and the civilian public, might have confidence in our efforts. It was a proud moment!

❦

Pleased to display the glory of the Service, I learned to be selective about footgear; practiced the little tricks to relax the sole area that allowed me to finish with a grin instead of a groan. I became conscious of the defensive care of the foundations that carried me through these extended walks. There were sizzling summer marches, chilling winter ones and those in a damp drizzle, some over dirt surfaces, grasses (cut low and high), paved roads and bumpy terrain.

Albeit with the most thoughtful podiatric preparation, the route on this July the Fourth felt nine miles long in the region of my arches. In actuality it was a mile—but because the terrain of Seattle is sharply up hill and down dale, it seemed endless as we strode in proper military cadence.

Another consideration was the music; for instance, during the course of any march we strained to keep in time. There was always a band in advance "somewhere," and one "somewhere" several companies behind with each of these playing a different tune at a dissimilar rhythm, whilst we kept a steady stride of our own behind our Detachment officers who were out front setting the pace.

For certain occasions a variety of talents had to be developed such as when we walked behind the mounted troops where we uniformed forces toiled to keep a proper tempo, and also side-step the unselfconscious horse-droppings without moving out of line or missing a beat! One was asked to be a "soldier" in every sense of the word!

To be a member of a parade, a consciousness of fraternity is a requirement—the sense of belonging, the feeling that all are pulling together to perform in unison. It means being on an agreeable wavelength with your neighbor, and the opportunity to experience the sensation of "oneness" that ripples back and forth through the lines like the movements of the flags that fly in the breezes before and behind. When the display is over, the last corner turned, the final "Company, Halt!—Parade Rest!—Break Ranks!" is said, then there is a relaxation of tenseness, and a tremor of shared exhilaration and pride that is felt for hours afterward.

❦

We arrived in Seattle at the beginning of June, the Fourth of July celebration had come and gone and the summer was upon us. Due to the thoughtfulness of Lieutenant Stoller, arrangements were made to take interested members of the company to a convenient place for swimming on weekends.

Bathing, the Army way, was one of the activities that

brought home to us the fact that we were Government Property—that is, we moved to the lake like a bivouac party. Fatigue dresses or raincoats covered our swim suits (non-Army issue), and we rode in the trucks in convoy order with our recreational needs. We were accompanied by a separate vehicle that contained our Mess crew and the gear required to feed us picnic style. Our company commander, who remained properly dressed in her uniform, helped set out the meal for her girls, then retired to the background like the scenery. At the end of the day, heads were counted and we returned in the same order in which we arrived.

At the lakeside this course might have inhibited socializing, flirting and high-jinks on the part of the conservative because male enlisted and commissioned personnel were there too, but since there was no insignia to be seen on any beach attire and the less timid will always "find a way," those enlisted and commissioned people always "found a way."

Routine claimed us in the way we boarded the trucks every day for the journey from Fort Lawton to the Port area. I had grown accustomed to the Post where evenings were spent either in writing, laundering, fellowship, duty in the barracks or other occupations, so that before I realized it, six months had gone by. It was mid-August and time for my first furlough.

This was to be my initial crossing of the country on my own, sans the companionship of my female group and without transportation, meals and sleeping quarters arranged for me. There were no roomettes or compartments available on the trains, and if there were, they did not fit into my economy. My ticket called for a coach seat, upright in the light of day, lowered to a half-reclining position in the dimness of the evening; naps to be garnered half prone and fully clothed, for four nights and three days. My luggage consisted of a modest valise that held folded cotton skirts, shirts, ties, lingerie, shoes and sundries. I carried separately, a winter outfit to face the fall weather in.

Aboard the train I found people anxious to talk about their loved ones in the Armed Forces, and servicemen who concerned for themselves, looked for a willing ear to tell it to, and mine was "it" since I was in uniform too. Other passengers were intrigued with women in the WAAC so conversation started before I settled into my seat. For some, the verbal exchanges never stopped—they continued through the dark of night. Slumber was grabbed in snatches.

There was a camaraderie amongst the riders; one loaned another a jacket for cover if the night chill was penetrating, if other needs appeared, passengers shared whatever they had. Food was a comfort when lack of sleep threatened fatigue, and a bountiful appetite gave me the energy to face each new dawn. I changed into a fresh shirt and skirt every day from my provident little piece of luggage and was complimented on my crisp military appearance which was pleasing since I was ever conscious of how I represented the Corps.

Four restless nights and several transit changes later, I arrived in a groggy state at Grand Central Station, where Dad greeted me warmly. I had to be firmly escorted, but presented the brightest expression I could muster while I labored to keep myself in the proper upright military posture. We took more transports to our bungalow home in Long Island, where, too tired to speak, I fell asleep.

I opened my eyes briefly and saw my sister Ruth examining my uniform curiously then awakened a day and a half later, ready to commence the vacation part of my furlough, and when I dove into the food Mother had prepared on my request, the family heaved a sigh of relief at the sight, for it was "old times" in regard to my famous appetite.

Fare Thee Well—
Dear Barracks,
Dear Goddess,
Dear Auxiliary

On my return to Fort Lawton there were changes under discussion. We were abuzz with the rumor that we might be moved into a hotel in Seattle to be nearer our work at the Port!

Soon orders were posted and what had been whispered, became fact, but before we moved out of the Fort, we were taken to the Stratford Hotel to scrub the premises. It was an old establishment whose interior of stained walls, musty furnishings and faded carpeting, all long neglected, necessitated a thorough overhaul.

We made several trips to town in our fatigues, accompanied by pails, soaps, mops, brushes, vacuums, etc. We scoured, and the Fort Lawton "bug squad" sprayed; old papered walls were dusted, carpets and woodwork washed, draperies removed, cleaned and rehung.

Hotel beds were replaced by regulation cots made up with Army linen and blankets and with footlockers properly positioned; the hotel desks, mirrors and night tables remained. Each room had a smaller or larger bath which completed the sensation of wild extravagance! Scrubbed, sanitized, dowdy but clean, we moved in with a city address:

WAAC Headquarters Detachment
Port of Embarkation
Stratford Hotel
Seattle, Washington

At a later date I illustrated our unique mode of decor for a news article written on military life in a hotel—but for the present we were out of the shared barracks and into individual rooms, and depending upon the spaces—lodged alone or several women were quartered together. In my case, my assignment allowed me the area to myself. The accommodations were modest in size, but the luxury was overwhelming!

A public telephone was installed on each floor—when it rang the person nearest to it answered and screamed for the recipient of the call in uninhibited style. The usual hotel keys that assured individual retirement for guests were not issued to us since we lived by an "open portal" policy with unlocked doors closed only during sleeping hours or for any temporary needs. Our lives and possessions were laid bare for inspection every day.

Even with the advantage of private rooms, baths and a phone on every floor, our place of residence had a serious disadvantage—an absence of "necking" places! On the ground floor there were no secluded corners for good-night kisses which the Fort barracks had in profusion—on returning from dates we had to be inventive!

❦

No sooner had we settled into town when we were again ablaze with rumor. Another transposition was in the wind for our company and every member of the Women's Army Auxiliary Corps: The question was—would we and could we become members of the Army of the United States proper! We could—and would! By act of Congress, we were shortly to be a part of the soldiery—not an "auxiliary" branch. This meant that we might be discharged from the WAAC and go home, or be sworn into the new Women's Army Corps with attendant privileges, rules and regulations. For weeks gossip was rampant with "what ifs," the pros and cons, and what our personal decisions would be! I had no doubt where I stood—I had entered the Military for the duration.

In late September we were offered the final option of continuing in, or separating from, the Service. Some accepted the choice of leaving, while the remainder of us elected to be sworn into the Army en masse after the first of October 1943, when the law would go into effect.

We members of the WAAC wore the mythical likeness of Athena, the Grecian goddess of war and victory, on our uniform insignia because she was the lady who lent her distinction and protection to us. It was a unique association, and now the time had come to say goodbye to her as well as to our auxiliary status. The Congressional act that made us members of the Army, changed the special WAAC eagle design on our hats, to the eagle worn by the men, and our lapel ornaments and shoulder patches to the command or corps that we were part of.

The swearing in ceremony took place on a sunny 8th of October at the Port in an open site, after which we were welcomed to our new estate by our Commanding General, Eley Denson, with an audience of other military and civilians who could spare the time to attend. The army band played the appropriate martial music for the event up to the moment the formalities were concluded—then with a nod from one of the officers, the band broke into "You're in the Army Now!" The solemn mien of all was slowly replaced by smiles that grew broader as the serenade progressed and ended in laughter when that tune was followed by "Oh How I Hate to Get Up in the Morning!" In contrast to the sun and fun of that proud day, we received the insignia of the Transportation Corps a week later at Fort Lawton in a drizzling rain!

I was now no more Auxiliary First Class, but Private First Class.

The realization that I was "Army" was brought home to me when we were granted the privilege of free mail but I was not entirely convinced my first stampless letter marked "Free" would arrive at my parents' home—it did, which bolstered my confidence in using the system thereafter.

There were other happy secondary effects derived from

our changeover, for instance, when additional winter outfits arrived for our group, I noted the cloth, color and fit were inferior to those worn by the ladies around me who had joined the Corps earlier than I. While the war progressed, there were compromises made in the fabric and workmanship, thus problems developed in the manufacture. We, who came in later entertained no grandiose expectations such as a skirt that matched the jacket, but were content with near-matches of the approximate materials. The opportunity for some of us to own an alternate suit of a fine quality presented itself when the Auxiliary Corps was in the process of conversion.

When anyone left the Service, all equipment given to enlisted personnel was collected by the Quartermaster Department, with the exception of one set of clothing to wear home. At that period many of the pieces of returned wardrobe were the earliest of their kind, so one way of obtaining something with the desired tailoring was to find a departing soldier who wore the exact size, earmark it for oneself, then request that suit or separate parts. Any turned-back stock was eagerly received when reissued because we could have not only uniforms, but other trappings missing from our official lists. Under this system I received my second winter dress items, a part of the prized, though wearied, original lot that were of like shade and make—a bonus over and above the ordinary.

The fact that these outfits did not come with two skirts like the proverbial blue serge suit, made for a fragile seat in that part of this second-hand treasure of mine, therefore I wore the skirt tenderly and sparingly and monitored the threads very carefully, lest they part company at an inopportune moment. Subsequently I made unsuccessful attempts to purchase replacements on a par with those custom tailored "hand-me-downs"—my proud cast-offs, which were worn to threadbare glory by discharge time.

More aspects of our dressing questions were present than met the eye. In Basic Training clothing for the day was based on the program and the weather, but at other stations, all dressed according to orders as seasonal changes occurred. There were variations allowed on the outer garments—for instance, in the winter months, the option to wear a blouse/jacket under the raincoat (with removable lining) or the overcoat, according to personal comfort. When away from a Post, discretion guided these choices.

For the female members in the Military, the donning of the uniform had its accompanying subtleties in the grand plan of the Women's Army Corps. The fact that the same skirt, shirt, blouse, hat, purse, raincoat, overcoat, and shoe was common to us all, the problem of the day's costume should have been eliminated, and was—except for the rules of femininity which retained their time honored place!—so that "What shall I wear this morning" was as pertinent to Service dress as it had been in civilian life. One soon had a favorite shirt, a preferred skirt or shoe, and kind of hosiery or type of headgear to choose from. Options even extended to the tie and how to wear it—we could tuck it in between the second and third button of the shirt, or let it hang loose.

An off-duty dress in shirtwaist style was distributed eventually, which created an excuse for a spectator pump to accompany it for a less severe effect. We then could express the fancy for a particular shirt, skirt, tie, blouse, dress, or coat and have a selection of millinery, and footwear!

So, the question of "What shall I wear today" remained . . . . Ah, Me!! Girls will be girls!

THE BIG TOWN

In a more serious vein, our loyalties were now divided. We Army people, taking root at the Stratford Hotel, had one foot in the city and with the other, would keep a toehold on Fort Lawton where we had wants to be looked after, for when sick call, toothache or hospital care beckoned, they needed to be attended to by the Medical and Dental staffs in a familiar khaki atmosphere. We would also lack the feeling of companionship at the sight of soldiers strolling in the evening, milling about the Service Club, the PX, Post Office, theater or other places where life was lived after the working day. Even chapel services seemed promising as an excuse to visit our old haunts.

Because we were now "town folk," there were more features of the Fort and barracks we would miss; among them was the uninterrupted view of Puget Sound, where in the evenings we placed chairs on a platform outside the rear door, and watched the sundown in its ever changing glory. It then became apparent, that in order to participate in the above-mentioned benefits and socialities, we would be frequent passengers on the Post buses as they made their bumpy way between Seattle and Fort Lawton.

❦

While we settled into the hotel part of our living, we

had the permission of our commanding officer to decorate our quarters in any way that pleased us with Military guidelines to be observed.

Adding the personal touch to my lodging was an extension of my artistic inclinations which resulted in a more colorful "home away from home" and satisfied the nesting instinct. Now that I was six and a half months in the service and in my fourth location, I could have made myself comfortable in my footlocker if circumstance demanded. Since I was now able to expand, I became busy with paste, paper, cardboard and sample wallpaper patterns, family photos, and prints of ballet stars, then placed my finds of old china here and there. Mosquito netting was purchased for curtains, embellished with ruffled edges and hung from the top of the window to cover it completely and block the view, which "view" was a brick wall. It was told to me later that my room was shown to visitors who came to see how Army life was lived in a hotel!

❦

After we were established, a serious problem manifested itself; we found that we ladies were not welcome everywhere in the city because this area, adjacent to Bremerton, Washington, was considered old Navy territory. In Seattle the concept of female soldiers was new. Our girls returned from shopping tours with stories of being rudely ignored—for instance standing at store counters where everyone was waited on but they. In discourses concerning this at our quarters, it was decided the unfriendly attitude was due to resistance to any but Navy personnel and the human factor of envy since we looked so spanking smart in our uniforms. Gradually the citizens grew accustomed to us as we went about our business. Later, when I looked for unusual supplies for shows, weddings and parties, residents and storekeepers received me graciously, and generously donated articles to assist my plans.

In Seattle, weekly meetings at the Detachment included news of interest to us such as speakers on current events, history and medicine with emphasis on personal hygiene and other problems of social interchange. Suggestions were welcomed about subjects to be discussed or topics of interest to all. Some girls worked other than daytime hours and they were considerately informed of company news. At one gathering, Lieutenant Stoller found a warm response to her offer to teach a language class, which started our lessons in beginner's Spanish.

During one of the forementioned sessions, we were given examples of enemy propaganda of the type used against women in the services. Tales were disseminated not only within our own country to discredit the female members of the Armed Forces with regard to our moral standards and habits, but stories drifted back to us from overseas military locations where the Axis powers sought to weaken the esprit of the ranks there too.

While we spread about the country into the soldier domain, there was resistance to the WAC on the part of some male personnel and instant acceptance by others. We also had to make a place for ourselves with the members of the Regular Army, the careermen who hoped to ignore our presence in "their" war and with whom we had to find a level of existence, the subject of which was the basis for an amusing and paradoxical incident that took place during a routine day at one Port office.

An old-line Master Sergeant in charge of a particular office had as little to do with "the new-fangled female Army" as he could, other than to conduct his business. One day in his presence a male officer reprimanded an enlisted woman for over-staying her lunch hour and accused her of taking liberties. The old timer stepped in and quoted by rule, number, and line what that WAC was entitled to. Fair was fair to him and he wasn't going to have *his* personnel abused, male or female, when they were in the right. We were there to stay and eventually were integrated into the various required duties without being looked at askance. We continued to make inroads into our new world where we showed by example that we were serious, hard-working ladies bound by a common purpose with both the military and civilian residents of the area.

If the people in Seattle had modifications to make in their impressions, we did too in a different way regarding the local weather which changed naturally with the seasons. The well-known rainy period came as a matter of course to the Washingtonians—but to members of my Detachment who came from elsewhere, it was no routine affair. Equipped with galoshes and hooded raincoats, we covered our clothes and feet at the appropriate times until the "appropriate" times occurred at intervals all day—every day. Putting on and taking off the shoe coverings and coats, and throwing our hoods over and off our hats became tiresome enough for us to think about changing our habits. After a period we did what the natives did, we sloshed through the rain sans galoshes and extra head coverings and adopted the attitude that the drops could fall where they might, and who cared—not we!

The snow season that we from the Northeast were accustomed to, was seen in the distance atop Mt. Olympus where the white-capped peaks gave the nostalgic look and feel of "home" with the added advantage of not having to get out the snow shovel.

ॐ

When the general direction of my talents became known to my Commanding Officer, I became the unofficial company Special Service person, while I continued my regular job at the Port of Embarkation. The work included decorating for appropriate occasions, making party arrangements, and planning the details for the wedding of one of our enlisted women at the request of Lieutenant Stoller, the ceremony to be held in our hotel lounge at a later date.

This was in the fall of the year and it was the season of the Jewish High Holy Days for which occasion we were invited to attend services at local houses of worship. First came the Old Testament New Year, "Rosh Hashanah," followed in nine days by the Day of Atonement, "Yom Kippur," at which time it is customary to fast for the day, and I did.

After each of these services I was asked to be a guest at the home of a member-family of the synagogue where as a female in the Military, I was an object of curiosity. The WAC was much admired, my hosts and other guests complimented my uniform, were interested in the details of my day and praised the contributions I and the others might be making to the war effort. It was heartwarming to be entertained and appreciated in this way since I lived detached from the civilian life I had left. Within our own quarters, none found a need to appraise their own patriotism since our very presence there was the answer to why we were gathered together.

A light mood prevailed following these religious holidays because Halloween was approaching, and with pumpkin pie and demons in the wings, my Company Commander requested that I do some morale building. It was decided that a group would go on a hunt for decorations from the fields and farms, while I designed and constructed a fitting background for the interior of our dining area.

When the women reappeared toting stalks of Indian corn and pumpkins, the Mess Hall was transformed into a haunted retreat. With the assistance of my volunteer committee, shimmering ghosts, witches, and goblins appeared, which apparitions then floated about and peered from between the cornstalks in the flickering shadows of the candlelight. At the evening meal, a "hard day at the war office" could be put aside and the spirit of Halloween enjoyed by us and our guests.

In the case of the wedding, Lieutenant Stoller and I conferred. She thoughtfully proposed to sponsor the service and festivities as a gift to the bride and groom. I outlined my needs then canvassed the downtown area for the decorative crepe papers, ornaments, flowers, and trimmings to suit my designs. Generous storekeepers gave me items they had hoarded because everything was in short supply. Civilian friends loaned table linens and candelabra, our cooks baked the elaborate wedding cake, set out dainty sandwiches and sparkling punch, and we supplied the guests—military and non service—who filled the room.

On that Saturday afternoon in November, accompanied by the soft strains of nuptial music, the uniformed couple stood happily in front of the fireplace in our Day Room amidst the dazzle of white, gold and silver crepe papers and the reflection from the ribbon bows and wedding bells that encircled the room. In the background, the buffet table was set with a many-tiered cake on a lacy cloth, glistening silverware and white napery. Donations of greenery filled many bowls, the room was polished, all the soldiery's buttons and insignias shown brightly, and their shoes were buffed to a turn. It presented an affecting, beautiful and sentimental sight—this our first gala occasion that brought a tear to every eye! An Army Chaplain performed the ceremony, General Denson gave the bride away. The cake cutting and toasts that followed completed the joyous gathering and the happy couple left for their honeymoon.

On Sunday, while bathing in the pleasant afterglow, I found it especially amusing, and Lieutenant Stoller startling, that the total cost to her for the glittering celebration was $10! Then from the sublime to the ridiculous—it was back to the "salt mines" on Monday morning, when up to my elbows in soap suds, I took my turn at KP.

❦

There was good news about the progress of the War this early part of November, consequently the illumination in homes and stores, on streets, billboards and on theater marquees, which had been extinguished at twilight lest they be a target for enemy attack, were ablaze again in honor of heartening reports. Several of us stood at our windows above the main floor and stared at the dazzle of the theater lights across the street as they blinked on and off again to celebrate their rekindled life.

This month government insurance was offered and I took advantage of the reasonable rates and too, wool scarves were distributed to us, therefore the one I was knitting for myself I gave to a serviceman, then continued making more of them for the male soldiers who were not issued any. At this time I was delighted to have two new pairs of regulation shoes due to the difficulty in acquiring supplies and the narrow width of my feet.

During this November I received the first photo of my brother Leonard in uniform. Even though I was proud of him, my female soul was touched, and my mother instincts all raced to take their protective place, in which case I worked more industriously because I hoped to get the War over with successfully and sooner, to bring Leonard and all other brothers, fathers, sons, sweethearts and friends back home.

How many women in the Forces thought the same thing! Unrealistic, but true!

Inasmuch as I spent my early twenties in the Military, I reflected the usual age concern about weight-watching although I had no problem in this sphere, and did not allow such a consideration to interfere with my general enjoyment of any foods—especially the gifts of "goodies" sent to me by family and friends. Fortunately, my eating habits included quantities of protein, and in addition, I harbored the instincts of a rabbit in regard to vegetables which were a treat for me. Allowed ungoverned selection on the mess line, my choices were lean ones—and because we could eat all we wanted, the dining hours were pleasant enough for me—but not for all!

Until early 1944, we were served menus long established through the history of the Service, and tailored to the needs of male soldiers in all stages of duty. This plan (later adjusted), produced a number of overweight women, whose well-being and efficiency were of concern to the Army. A directive came through to the effect that those beyond a certain scale evaluation, were to make an effort to correct the circumstance which would improve their health and general outlines, and thence their productivity in the war effort. This caused a ripple of comment through our entire residence and some re-evaluation of dining habits—but in the long range hardly any changes in the said contours!

To go back to the generous portions provided us and the freedom to eat whatever we saw fit, there was thoughtless waste too. I well remember a fellow volunteer who put eight spoons of sugar in her average cup of coffee—and I subsequently noticed the unstirred sugar in the bottom of the cup when she drained the liquid. I noted that she was the exception, not the rule, and wondered if she had observed the sign posted in the dining room that said "TAKE ALL YOU WANT—BUT EAT ALL YOU TAKE."

I must mention here one of the pleasures at the Seattle detachment was the mess crew under the direction of Sergeant Frances Pestrak. They were magnificent cooks and turned the food provided us into "Queenly" fare. I held them in high esteem, but never paused too long in admiration because I was busy eating when mealtime came around. The cream puffs were delectable and it was not unusual for me to down six of these desserts after very generous main courses. The reputation of these cooks traveled through the ranks of our friends in the male sector, who curried favor with us in the hope of an invitation to dinner. We were allowed guests, provided reservations were made for them and seating was available that evening in the hotel dining room.

When a troopship left the Port of Embarkation for far

places, the area meat supply went with them, it was then that our diet was fish for a few days and since we were in the region where salmon was plentiful, it was often on our table. This suited my taste, for such imagination did our cooks display withal, that most of us rushed home for "Mom" Pestrak's good cookin'. In fact our kitchen team was the inspiration for honoring holidays and other occasions with flair. They could be so innovative with Army rations, that they were the excuse for Mess Hall participation in rounding out our preparations for detachment entertainment!

In my Special Service work I had the assistance of Delsie Hill, a fellow WAC, a willing and able addition to my plans. Before a project commenced, volunteers were called for to assist me and many hands shot into the air, which impressed the officers and meant credits toward the esprit de corps of those who proffered. When the time came to commence work, few turned up for any length of time, but Delsie shared all tasks with me to the end.

For each scheme, the necessary materials were garnered, then we cut, sewed, pasted and mounted. I enjoyed supplying an atmosphere of cheer and tried to be original, yet appropriate when I formed my ideas. Upon being requested to create a background for the coming Thanksgiving feast, I met the challenge with my faithful committee buoyed by confidence in our creative kitchen. Happily, the Mess Hall was spacious and lent itself suitably for dinners, dances, shows and general rejoicing; alternatively, our hotel lounge (in Army parlance, the Day Room) was utilized too, since it was large and homey.

For this commemoration I needed pup tents, the kind used for bivouac. I visited with General Denson who always seemed pleased when he could do something for us and he saw to it that we had the needed items. They were then disguised with branches and other camouflage to simulate Indian tepees!

Cornstalks again graced the Mess Hall as they had at Halloween time. I planned too a mural of trees where amid the trunks Indian and Pilgrim children played a game of tag while other girls and boys peeked flirtatiously at one another from behind the foliage and Indian Braves with hatchets chased fleeing, squawking turkeys intended for the roasting pans. The tables boasted miniatures of all these themes.

Before Christmas and the New Year, we brought in holly leaves and berries; these by courtesy of civilian friends who invited us to pick from the grounds about their homes where the greenery grew in profusion. Here the theme was seraphim with halos and wings aglitter as they tiptoed through the blue sky and billowing clouds, while stars twinkled among them against a backdrop of bedsheets that lined the room. Table settings, lit by candlelight for several evenings of the holiday, gave all a heavenly feeling. For the New Year, I added seasonal greetings amidst the angels!

The *Seattle Star* printed a photograph on the front page that showed the decorations in progress as I prepared the dining area for the season's celebration and dance. They published, too, a New Year photograph, posed by one of my friends, Agnes Clinkscale, which was an example of the publicity shots produced by the Army Signal Corps and for whom I selected one of our WACs, applied the correct studio makeup, and planned the layout. The photographic work was done by Technical Sergeant Marvin Richmond, a member of the POE Signal Corps Photo Section, and with whom I worked compatibly and often.

I was privileged to enjoy the confidence of my Detachment Officers, with the result that the ideas I conceived were not monitored in any way. Whatever I could accumulate the wherewithal for, I was given the liberty to do—happily there was little expense to the United States Army. Anything that scissors, paint, glue, glitter, crepe paper, poster board, cloth, Army supplies and civilian donations could do to further my creativity, was encouraged with cooperation and praise. All these opportunities for morale building we could afford to indulge in because the results showed more in the effort, than monetary outlay, and even allowed us the freedom to invite guests. In grim times these remembrances took on more gayety, provided a break in the work, worries and tensions of war, and brought home to me what was really meant by Special Service. This made it all worthwhile.

I spent full time at my job and labored afterward at the Stratford Hotel, and when necessary, the other women did extra duty too. Our officers saw to it that we put in a reasonable day, but if various matters required overtime, there was no question as to whether the need would be filled because wars are not fought in nine-hour shifts! At our headquarters, Lieutenants Ida Stoller and Wilhemina Hinton were ever on call for us and we wondered when these women slept, so attentive were they to our requirements. Holidays were also circumstances when their great thoughtfulness came to the fore.

On Christmas morning, socks filled with fruit, nuts and candy hung on every door and at this particular time when apparel, like everything else, was scarce, our officers gave each woman a pair of hosiery. This was luxury on a grand scale. In return, our choices for them were carefully selected to enhance their special interests.

In anticipation of Christmas and Chanukoh (the latter the Hebrew Feast of Lights), when packages started to arrive in the mail, we cautioned one another about sneaking a glance! We pressed, guessed, squeezed and speculated on each parcel and satisfied our curiosity when we opened a few items prematurely and saved the rest for the appropriate moment. When the happy time came, the goodies and presents were shared with friends. We exchanged gifts with one another around our huge tree in the Day Room for which we made our own decorations. It didn't take much for us to create a festive event with modest means as we were accustomed to extending our little to cover a sizeable area.

Weeks before, I shopped for novelties in miniature form and found books, packs of wee playing cards, small checker games, little harmonicas, dice, writing papers and pens, sweets and treats, all of which I packaged and sent overseas. The quest for these Lilliputian particulars opened a world in minutiae because my purpose was to please, but not burden the fighting men. I wondered where friends and loved ones would be when each opened his packet.

The Cheery, The Eerie, The Sad, Glad And Bad!

When one of our WACs formed a friendship that progressed through the romance stages to engagement and marriage, we rejoiced with one another.

Weddings were planned according to the preferences of the parties involved. There were ceremonies held at our Post Chapel, nuptials performed at a civilian friend's home, those the women preferred to have in their home towns surrounded by their nearest and dearest, and then there was the one held in our hotel Headquarters. The latter was an affair to which the whole Company was invited to celebrate with the bridal couple. There were not many marriages among members of our unit, just a treasured few.

Wartime unions that involved parties in the Military had a particular urgency, especially those in the desperation of immediate separation like the one in which Margie Molland and I participated.

On one visit to Fort Lawton, we peered into the dimly lit Army chapel where the Chaplain and an about-to-be-married couple stood before the altar. The groom was a soldier, the bride, a girl who had traveled far and alone to become his wife before he went overseas. She was dressed in her marriage finery; the pretty dress now a mass of wrinkles from the close confines of her luggage, her crumpled hat and crushed shoes resurrected as best they could be—and in her gloved hands she carried a fresh nosegay.

The Chaplain spied Marge and me and requested us to be witnesses, which service we willingly performed for these two unattended lovers. Afterwards we invited them to dinner, where the cheerfulness of a pleasant restaurant was a contrast to the dreariness and loneliness of the empty chapel. There was much to tug at the heart at such a time, an ocean of tears to be blinked away before they poured down our cheeks. There were, on other occasions more heart-rending occurrences brought on by the horrors of War!

Our group went through happy times or crises together and during the desolate ones there were many shoulders to unburden oneself on. Depending on the amity formed, we could discuss various problems with those we felt would give the best advice or lend an ear, or if it were happy news, be elated with us. There were always over a hundred "sisters" to choose from, officers included.

What did we do on the days when one of our girls received a report that a husband, brother, father, or sweetheart was wounded, killed, or missing in action and she was faced with a wall of frustration, not knowing—not being able to "do" for a loved one in the terror of the hour? At those moments, tidings traveled through the Company like lightning; we gathered around the affected friend with words or an unspoken closeness. Each one comforted in her own way and saw to it that our companion in extremity was not alone—that we were stricken with her, and wished her grief were less. We did what we could.

❦

Did we have time for laughter?

When we had unscheduled evenings, dateless or laundry nights, or those free of duties—we had gab fests and traded thoughts about families, overseas or state-side relations, sweethearts, dates and mundanes, such as work. We talked in groups of two or three, or a crowd gathered in one room.

During one of these evenings, a friend said that we wouldn't be here forever and after we were discharged we'd be "buddies." This conjured up pictures of older men vet-

erans we knew from World War I with stories of their buddies. We had a range of looks on our faces from quizzical
to comic . . . buddies? were we going to be sitting around
"hoisting a few" in our T-shirts and fat bellies— remem-
bering The War? This caused much hilarity and hearty
shouts of "Hey, you're my buddy!" and we burst into song—
you guessed it . . . "My B u u d d d y . . . !"

At other confabs, the subject was Alaska and the probability of our moving there which was ever in the back of
our thoughts. Such discussions were based on Latrine Rumor—that thriving, time honored military avocation.
Stationed so far northwest one grew accustomed to the very
idea of our closeness to the Canadian and Alaskan domain.
Seattle families spoke familiarly of their vacation homes
on the Canadian West Coast or in the lower reaches of
Alaska. In my case my work put me on friendly terms with
the Aleutian region and also there was my personal concern
with Private Danny Glaubman who introduced himself to
me after I arrived at Fort Lawton, and was now at an
Army base on one of the Islands. For all of the foregoing
reasons, it was naturally assumed by us that we would be
the first personnel of the Women's Army Corps to join the
men that were posted there.

In preparation for assignment out of the United States,
we received training at the YMCA with self defense taught
by a member of the police force, and swimming and life
saving instruction by a Red Cross coach. Despite the overseas practice, and our growing familiarity with this Pacific
Northwest corner of our hemisphere, the expected move
toward Alaska never did materialize—instead, singly, or
in groups we were later dispatched to other stations in
or out of the country. For the immediate time being, in
town we stayed, and in Seattle life continued for us, cen-
tered around the Port and the Stratford Hotel.

❦

Our quarters were situated on a commercial street with other buildings that housed lesser businesses. My aforementioned room with its limited vista, faced the side wall of the building next door; between us were fire escapes and an alley.

One evening I discovered there was a window in this neighboring building, located at my level but a number of feet to the right, and I found with the proper tilt of my head I could peer into the room. What I witnessed was an eerie spectacle that startled me and piqued my curiosity. I saw women in loose white gowns, who carried candles, the only light in the room. They walked in a large circle around a central lectern from which a tall, white-haired theatrical-looking man directed the action and their choral chantings. An unearthly glow reflected on the faces of the male audience that lined the walls. The haunting incantations, flickering beams and moving shadows were other-worldly.

This was too exciting to keep to myself! When word was spread amongst a selected few, we crept quietly onto the dark seclusion of the fire escape and watched these rituals. Although we never did discover the meaning of the occult ceremonies, we revelled in the shows and enjoyed speculating about them because they were in direct contrast to a world of women whose lives were occupied with, and dedicated to, bringing the misery of our country's conflict to a close, and whose hours spent in this effort were an open book to be examined in any light. The subject of light and trust as opposed to shady activities is reflected too in the following incident.

The Military permitted our own service people or those of our allies to be housed and fed at any available Army installation, so that any soldier away from his or her station, or enroute, could take advantage of this hospitality. Canadian, English, Australian or members of the other Allied forces strolled about our Posts and appeared in our service clubs. Under the circumstances of this friendly exchange, a lady dressed in the uniform of a Canadian officer requested lodging for the night at the Stratford Hotel and was asked to share a room with one of our girls. She was gone in the very early morning with jewelry and money that belonged to her room-mate of the night before as well as possessions of other personnel housed on the same floor.

Trusting we were, and betrayed we were too—the War allowed no respite from human frailties!

The above event was not usual for us. What was a usual day at the WAC Detachment at the Stratford Hotel?

LIFE AT THE STRATFORD

The day at our quarters started at 6:30 A.M. as we were shocked out of our sleep with shouts of "Rise and Shine," "Time to Fall Out" and other stimulating phrases guaranteed to activate us—at which signal we threw on a robe or pieces of uniform; any parts of our pajamas that might show, we rolled up.

We stepped outside our rooms on each floor, aligned ourselves with our neighbors and answered to roll call. Physically, we were "here" as we stood at attention with eyes wide open—mentally, we were asleep in an upright position. After the First Sergeant's report that "All are present and accounted for Ma'am," we were dismissed by the officer in charge and straggled back to our rooms to get washed and dressed for breakfast. Raiment at this point, was anything comfortable since it was just us girls.

The tempo picked up while bodies flew past one another on the way to this first meal of the day. Food was stowed with one eye on the clock, then work lists were scanned for chores which commenced immediately after "chow."

We straightened and checked our rooms, dressed for our jobs, then appeared on the ground floor where trucks awaited transportation to the Port area for those who wanted to ride. If we elected to use the Army vehicle, the gossiping, laughing and singing we did helped to awaken to the hours ahead and was a boon to the closeness we enjoyed. Those who chose to walk hustled to get an earlier start, in which case we talked companionably while we strode toward the docks. We had the same choices on our return.

With the exception of the Detachment officers, women on KP, and off-duty WACs, the hotel was abandoned. Riders went in convoy—that is, our khaki-colored conveyances, several at a time, proceeded one behind the other with headlights on, giving us an environment of protection with occasional adventure. The fact that we were obviously Armed Forces property enroute to our assigned duties, did not deter a civilian driver from moving into line between the vans one morning which resulted in our drivers stopping short, throwing us all helter skelter and causing an assortment of body bruises and cuts. We were given first-aid or wrapped in splints where necessary, and those that could, limped to work.

For the daily review of our quarters at the Stratford Hotel we had to have rooms and baths clean and in GI order. Many late day hours we scrubbed, arranged footlockers and saw to it that closet contents were organized according to regulations—ready to be seen at any time, except leisure hours, of course. Inspections were done after we left for work for reasons of expediency, and if anything was amiss, those names appeared on the gig list. Faces wore smiles or frowns, spirits rose or fell according to whether there were extra tasks listed on the bulletin board, and to note if evening plans were "shot" or not.

Ah, well, we were there to serve!

At work, lunch was brought to the Port from the hotel in trucks specially equipped with containers suitable for hot and cold provisions, and accompanied by the kitchen crew.

In that section of building designated for a Mess Hall we had our portable tables, folding chairs, compartmented trays, metal eating tools, cups with folding handles, even condiment containers, and our food was ladled onto the receptacles from behind the chow line. Photographs were taken during one of these repasts when Charles Laughton, the eminent actor, came to visit with us, joined us for lunch and literally "spilled the beans," on himself. We afterward sent him on his way, clean and neat again, with which process several of us assisted him.

We fortunate ladies had our edibles offered appetizingly with each kind placed separately in the recessed niches of the trays, which we were then able to eat as courses. This system was opposed to that of the men who complained that all the fare landed on theirs in an indistinguishable pile—which custom may be the origin for the term Mess!

Our hard-working WAC cooks were relieved of transporting these luncheons on Sunday when we were "at home," and like home, a pot of coffee was always on, or a snack was available in the refrigerator at any time.

To continue our day at the hotel, the duties included KP, in rotation, for which we were excused from Port work for the day to aid in meal preparation and cleanup. Kitchen Police had always been associated with enormous quantities of potatoes which required peeling, but this one chore was eliminated eventually when we were the recipients of a machine for the purpose. This ingenious device happily tossed the spuds until they were coatless, and when the process was finished, we scoured the machine.

The day's tasks involved cleaning the grease trap (Ugh!!), washing a Mount Everest pile of serving pieces and institutional-sized pots and pans, vegetable preparation, and the keeping of work areas in an immaculate and ready state. KP could be lightened by the camaraderie of the kitchen crew where it became a time for singing and snappy patter, but was also the type of job that paid us all thanklessly at the end of the day with "dish-pan" hands!

Additional functions at the Detachment were running the elevator morning and evening and CQ (Charge of Quarters). For the latter, we manned the Reception Desk after dinner where we greeted visitors, received telephone messages and dispatched them to the proper parties, and where members of the company signed "Out" after work hours and "In" when they came back, so that no one went unaccounted for by bed check time when the assignment ended. Responsibilities had their humane side like CQ duty, for if we returned with escorts, we could pop our heads in the door and sign the company book to make the curfew, then linger a few moments for a good night kiss or to whisper sweet nothings, while any WAC behind the desk for the evening looked the other way!

In turn there were meetings to attend, fire drills, or the chore of working off gigs; all these at the hotel. Off the premises were swimming, lifesaving and Judo lessons at the local Y. For me, Sundays were leisure days; no morning line-ups, no cleaning and polishings, no neatly arranged rooms, no clocks to watch, whereon I took advantage of the lack of schedule and tossed my clothes everywhere on Saturday nights—for the sheer luxury of awakening the following mornings in a vast untidy mess! . . . Wheeee. . . !

Any outside interests we could pursue in our free hours; there were dates, trips to the surrounding areas, dates, dancing, dates, dining out, theater, dates and anything else that could be indulged in, and we seemed to have managed all of these at one time or another.

Roommates and Friends

Time went by and the complement of women increased, so another bed was moved into my modest quarters and Ella Dalessandro, a friend from our days in Basic Training, came to be my roommate. Due to my special duties and sometimes extensive hours, I was one of the few who had not been sharing living space.

My companion, petite and kind, could not refuse an offer of male companionship, with the result that she sometimes made two appointments for the same evening whereon several of us would be called upon to offer suggestions on how to make plausible explanations to one fellow or another.

Although Ella returned just in time for curfew (and always hummed softly while she prepared for bed), she was up in the early morning, still humming, bright-eyed and bushy-tailed, and ready for work the next day! However much Ella was out she seemed to find time for scrubbing, so that many times all I saw of her was her rump while she scoured the bathroom floor which was her particular specialty. We teamed well, our area sparkled and my partner and I did too. We prided ourselves on the neatness and cleanliness of the room and on our personal appearance; but for me, I required more time at home for my laundering, tidying and grooming than did Ella, to obtain the desired results.

❦

Life was intimate in our hotel home, our cause united, and like any close friends we performed little services for one another.

In or out of uniform, we were still concerned with our female endowments on which subject a friend, Christine Glovan, appealed for ideas on how to make her fine hair more luxuriant. I remembered that Glover's Mange Cure put a full coat on canines, so it was claimed, and happily might do the same for Christine. She was game and willing to try the Mange Cure. Once or twice a week she dutifully sat while I poured the foul-smelling cure onto her hair and massaged her scalp—turning our habitat into a veterinary clinic.

We couldn't stand the odor, or even one another during these sessions and good-naturedly, our friends never complained. It was one for all and all for one—but since nothing sprouted quickly enough to be seen like the early buds in spring, the procedure was discontinued until we could find something else to bring some instant magical consequences.

"Abracadabra!"

❦

Through the support we gave and received, we in the WAC formed fulfilling friendships based on our common goals and personal interests. A companion, Sarah MacIntosh and I, both loved hunting for antiques, I for china and glass, and Sarah for pewter objects so that when we walked home from the Port area together after work, the stroll not only satisfied our inquisitiveness about Seattle, but led to finds of old bric-a-brac for our collections. An added sidelight and benefit of these evening strolls was the laundryman near the Port, who did our poplin shirts. This patriotic Chinese-American gentleman returned them to us in pristine condition for nine cents apiece because he wanted to feel that he contributed time and effort toward winning the War. We were the most appreciative beneficiaries, particularly since his excellent work was much admired and saved us the toil of doing our own. We kept our little triumph a secret from our compatriots who indulged in the luxury of having their shirts done nearer to the hotel at a cost of thirty-four cents each— complete with wrinkles and too much starch. For Sarah and me our evening walks enhanced our concord as well as added the extra delightful accompaniments!

ꝗ

It was due to the comradeship between Marjorie Molland and me that I was introduced to my first taste of ale—one must grow and mature. On the subject of drink and food, Marge and I, both from New York felt the lack of the accustomed delights and decided we had done without our bagels and lox long enough!

Marge, of Norwegian background, and I of mid-European, credited our ample height, glowing complexions, firm white teeth and general good health to our regular "chomping" on those delicious plump circles filled with heartwarming smoked ingredients such as the lox (smoked salmon), sturgeon, and white fish—all of these items embellished with cream cheese and Greek olives.

We hunted down the appropriate delicacy shop, and on the chosen evening stepped into the tiny store whose display included all of our beloved fare. We shortly became aware of the fact that the people who crowded about us waved ration books and we did not have any, alas! Our apparent expressions of dismay were taken note of, and several people proffered their coupons which we declined to use since we were abashed by their generosity. The conversation was overheard by the shop owner who asked us to step forward and announced that we could have anything we wanted without ration coupons. We refused again, and he insisted, while the audience urged us to accept. We couldn't make our rooting gallery and the proprieter unhappy, so we did accede to their urgings with profuse thanks all around—then literally flew back to our housing with the treasure hoard.

We maintained the dignity of our uniforms until we reached Marge's room where we hurriedly set a feast table, in this case it was an ironing board—draped for the glorious occasion with linen from the bath. The bagels were cut apart with the handiest tools we could grab, while, with utterances of the greatest delight, we stuffed them with the gifts of the gods. We two downed the treats in record time accompanied by several quarts of milk.

It is, of course, understood, one doesn't broadcast to the whole neighborhood about the acquisition of such rare prizes. . . . Not on your life!

❧

While Marge and I had in common the above familiarity with city living, we also shared our quarters with many women from other environments. Country girls and city cousins were learning from one another about differing modes of life.

Dry cleaning systems were a fact of larger-town experience, with Army posts providing them for our convenience, and I used these services regularly. This was not so with those whose care of their sturdy wool apparel had always been via the tubs at home because commercial cleaning establishments were not known in their locale. The laundry room thus became the setting for one of life's lessons on a day when I observed a barracks mate laboring at the ironing board in an effort to press her freshly washed woolen uniform skirt and lined jacket. My solicitous observation on the difficulties of self-laundering these garments brought the questioning response, "How else will they get done!" Indeed—I was enlightened on the matter of how some of us accomplished our exemplary military appearance.

... And Out Of
the Stratford

My work at the Port continued during the day and so did my Special Service undertakings at the Hotel Stratford, until later when I left that office to be placed on Detached Duty temporarily for a recruitment campaign. My co-workers in the POE Drafting Section consisted of three civilians and four other Servicemen. Sergeant Lilley and I, as previously mentioned, drew the maps, charts and graphs and the rest attended to various other paper work.

A memorable personality was our resident Serviceman "Sad Sack," our own Walter Mitty, whose desk was crammed with pills and potions which he regularly and earnestly consumed and which were dispensed to him on "Sick Call." On his return from these medical visits, any inquiry of concern elicited no definite reply relative to the nature of any ailment. According to the daily recital of his complaints, "Mr. Mitty" seemed to be affected by everything from the first call in the morning to the food at all meals, with lunch and supper always described as a diet of "sheep"—mutton was not his favorite chop. His barracks near the Port he labeled "The Mud Flats" and they were, according to him, the probable cause of his vague ills, flat feet and the present conflict! Since the gift of humor was a saving grace in this time of war, we suspected that he was planted by the Commander-In-Chief for the purpose of lending some wit to our work week.

During my tenure in the Drafting and Blueprint Section, we in the office, both Military and civilian, grew close and fond of one another. In our daily exchange of banter, a sample of the conversation went like this: "Have you been to the town of Victoria on Vancouver Island?" "No!" "No?! Well, you must go! The boat ride up the Strait is magnificent and Victoria is quaint! How about going for an overnight trip? Good! We'll *all* go!" And we did!

On this occasion we stayed at the Empress Hotel which was akin to visiting in England in a former century and I reveled in it! Raised in a family interested in antiques and curiosities, I purchased miniature English china as gifts for my mother and sisters.

By the time we boarded the ferry again and started our return to Seattle, we were closer for the experience. Considering the precarious time-frame, we basked in the warmth we felt for each other in the united cause, and even if the War was the basis for our bond, we, as a group, were fortunate to be putting our shoulders to the wheel in such compatible company.

❦

The mixed Service and civilian associations enriched me, but socializing solely with the uniformed establishment had its "in" responses, and these emotions could best be exercised at the Fort Lawton Service Club.

Because numbers of the boys long stationed in the Aleutian and Pacific Islands were sent to this Post for R&R (rest and relaxation), their presence created situations unique to the Military in wartime. Trained for jungle or guerrilla warfare, they feared for their lives; consequently, by habit, they carried knives in their belts or combat boots as needed to ply their trade, and most had been away from accustomed society for months or years. Where else would one enter an Enlisted Men's Club and hear a GI behind the cloakroom counter coaxing the aforementioned soldiers to "check your knives and daggers here, gentlemen." Few were willing to do so since it had become their way of life to carry these objects and to depend on them for their very existence. It was also the first time I had had contact with Army men from the Indian tribes. They loved to dance, and I loved to dance, and we could dance up a storm together to the music of the service bands.

The times when men were "restricted to the post" meant that the Service Club was one of the few places of relaxation they could attend seeing that they were on call to leave the United States for who knew where? In some cases, home addresses were given to me, then in carefully worded phrases, and divulging as little as possible, I wrote to their families. "He is looking and feeling fine and you will hear from him eventually. He sends you his love — ."

I worried and wondered and had a heavy heart!

In town, the USO Club presented an alternative place to visit. Again there were dancing, music and library rooms, writing desks, game areas, restaurant and social corners. It was here that I discovered the delectation of the Scottish bagpipers who came from Canada to entertain us, and where I learned to listen until I could discern the various tunes. "They all sound alike, don't they?"—Well I thought so too until then, when the colorful Canadians taught me the difference and fortunately for me, these rousing pipers appeared every few weeks.

At the Club, we women exchanged smile for smile with strange men who were no strangers. Navy, Army, Air Forces, Marines and Coast Guardsmen were constant reminders that we were "in there" together. Underneath the thin covering of comradeship, was the reality of why we were in uniform, and these lighter moments provided the propellent and determination for the next day's work. We talked or listened, danced and sipped sodas, and perhaps infused one another with a modicum of courage for whatever would come tomorrow.

Seattle, Washington 4 July 1943.

Clarice, Christmas/New Year's, 1943-44. Seattle Star.

Clarice with Lt. Oscar Dvoretz, February 14th, 1944.

The author—police "mug shot." Aberdeen, Washington, 1944.

Newspaper ad for recruitment campaign, 1944.

"The New Spring Hat" Illustration for recruitment campaign, State of Washington, 1944.

"The Mess Sergeant" Illustration for recruitment campaign, State of Washington, 1944.

"Change of Station" Illustration for Recruitment campaign, State of Washington, 1944.

"Morning Cleanup and Exercises" Illustration for recruitment campaign, State of Washington, 1944.

"The New Potato Peeler" Illustration for recruitment campaign, State of Washington, 1944.

"Going Overseas" Illustration for recruitment campaign, State of Washington, 1944.

YET ANOTHER YEAR

The commencement of the month of January, 1944, took on importance in our lives because it was a way of calculating the length of the War—that time gone by since we were free to be at home and hearth. Only in our own minds did we count the days subsequent to when we had last looked into the faces of old friends and dear hearts, for in our residence we invested little comment in speculation, or the passing of time. Our philosophy was one of quiet confidence.

It was at this juncture that I, Lieutenant Stoller, and a WAC Port of Embarkation officer, had a discussion about my extracurricular activities at our headquarters which enabled me to present the idea of Special Service work as a full-time position. There did not seem to be any official office that sponsored such activity for us nor was any such connection ever mentioned to me, for whatever diversions we had not created for ourselves, we did not have! When we parted, it was with the idea that they would look into the possibility of a permanent job for me, which consideration was gratifying because I thought of what could be accomplished that would reflect on my company from the standpoint of morale-building.

In this season, amongst other requests, I was contacted by the Public Relations staff that published the informal *Port Bulletin* and asked to draft a new logo to be used for a more ambitious newsletter about to be launched, and which did not as yet have a name. There was to be a contest for a title, my design would be used to present the initial issue and details to all personnel in the area.

I conceived the idea for the temporary heading in the form of a blindfolded American eagle soaring through a field of stars and facing a large question mark as he squawked to one and all "What's my name!" The sketch pleased the staff who featured it on the front of the first issue of the newspaper the following month.

After November, December and the New Year when the days were quiet and routine, I had the leisure to remind myself that a tooth needed to be attended to, which necessitated my presence at the Dental Clinic at Fort Lawton. I abhorred the thought of extensive care, fortunately found there was going to be little of it, but I still required several appointments. I grew not to mind the visits since the facility seemed to have the handsomest male attention any WAC could ask for. A session that required novocaine had two benefits: one—to deaden the pain and the other, the opportunity to exchange banter with the Dental officers who were "painless" to look at! A happy break in the work week!

During one such sitting, I was involved in a flirtation where everything seemed to be progressing satisfactorily with a date in the offing—when lo—I turned my head in the process of the work and stared into the eyes of one of my WAC officers, who as fate would have it, had her appointment at the very same hour! In this case, coincidence and inconvenience went hand in hand in the system of Army medical care, for the dental chairs were placed all in a row, in open style, without partitions.

Foiled in that situation, other opportunities for dalliance and sociality sprang eternal and in the spirit of fellowship, our Detachment received a blanket invitation to dinner followed by a show and dance hosted by soldiers from a neighboring air base. In the same warm humor, a number of us accepted the opportunity to be with another branch of the Armed Forces. The airmen sent a truck for us and we were off for the evening like Cinderellas where we were "wined and dined" in a manner of speaking—since the wine was not allowed at the mess. The complete party was made up of us, the airmen and Nurse Cadets.

Entertainment was composed of USO talent and local civilian residents who bravely paraded their offerings, mostly amateur, all of which were received by us with thunderous applause. The Military will respond with great appreciation for less than the best, while basking in the warmth of a well-meant effort. Afterward, we of the Services danced and enjoyed one another's company in our special closeness until the end of the evening. On our return, we WACs discussed the event, and the stage presentation in particular, put on the back burner an idea for a show of our own we thought we would like to do, tossed a few ideas about—and went to sleep.

❦

Several weeks into this new year, Detachment rumors circulated in regard to Lieutenant Stoller's possible reassignment, which hearsay turned out to be true. She had definitely been transferred, and since an order is an order, she prepared to go. All worked as a team in the Corps and adjusted to quick changes, with adaptability a prerequisite for joining the army life.

We speculated on the determinants for her change of station and any number came to mind. Had she requested overseas duty? Were her talents as a Commanding Officer needed elsewhere? Included in the theoretical list was the age-old perogative of the Army system: that anyone could be transferred for no cause whatsoever and "ours not to reason why. . . !"

Many of us indicated to her that we would miss an officer who so expertly balanced the welfare of her company with the needs of the War. We looked back on the hot days of summer when we were privileged to have those visits to the lake. Remembered, too, were the classes in Spanish for those who were interested, and her confrontations with the upper echelon officers, to ease our employment and acceptance as female soldiers. Brought to mind was the fact that when necessities were luxuries, each company member received a holiday surprise of precious hosiery, and we appreciated a leader who saw to it that we had new shoes in days of scarcities.

Personally, I was mindful of how we planned the decor for Halloween, Thanksgiving and Christmas to bring a lighter spirit into our living quarters in desolate times. I recalled, with pleasure, a Commander, who thoughtfully arranged a memorable wedding day for one of her own.

I promised to visit with her the following April at Fort Hamilton in Brooklyn, New York, where she expected to be stationed, then at the appointed time, a squad of us accompanied the Lieutenant to the railroad station and remained until the train screeched, lurched and belched its warning to us that it was about to depart—only then did we regretfully exit.

The Changing of the Guard

Vacancies are immediately filled in the Military and in a few days, Captain Dora Petmecky was installed to take over the duties as our Commandant. Under these circumstances, an alteration in atmosphere and management was to be expected and at a company meeting, our new Commanding Officer introduced herself to us with comments geared to those ends.

Like the proverbial "new broom," changes in our day now required us to rise and shine and appear in the lobby fifteen minutes earlier than usual. We were required to dress in our short- sleeved, short length, green and white seersucker fatigue dresses with matching panties and roller hats, ankle socks and sneakers for a "daily dozen." We went out to the parking lot and performed before an amused civilian audience on its way to early hour work. "Everybody on your toes—now bend over, 1-2-3-4!" This return to a basic training formula at the break of day gave way to some second thoughts on the part of the new administration, the exercise project was moved indoors and soon faded out of the morning picture entirely, to the relief of all.

We passed into other phases, and in the interest of one of them, I was summoned to the Detachment office for a chat with our Captain on the subjects of our colorless hotel entrance and dingy Day Room, and how we might obtain more inviting looks for both. These surroundings were a symphony in worn, faded tans and browns that reflected the olive drabness of our uniforms. The consensus was that a contrast would be welcome.

The ideas I suggested were happily received since they were within our economical range and would create the effect of warmth and relaxation. I canvassed for, and purchased our needs at prices that amounted to donations and the drapes and slipcovers were made by a professional, at a nominal charge. Ornaments about the room and entrance hall were painted and reconditioned which resulted in the desired effect on the morale of the Company.

❦

Women in uniform we were, and feminine we were too—the flowered chairs, decorations over the fireplace and pretty prints on the walls mirrored our inherent grace in the hours away from our war offices. Further evidence that our womanly senses needed to be catered to was the fact that perfumes were no strangers to our quarters since they sometimes adorned the hotel desks in our rooms; indeed there were powders, rouges and lipsticks in our medicine cabinets and purses. Hairstyles were changed to go with the current trends within reason of regulations (off the collar) and the outlines of the uniform headgear.

February brought with it early Spring displays of millinery in the store windows which as always, were a symphony of flowers, veils and feathers, on straw. A cluster of us strolled through a department store and did the womanly thing; we impulsively stopped and tried on the new season "look" for an amused audience of sales help and shoppers. There was good natured joshing all around during the time we sat in front of the mirrors and moved this way and that for the full effect, which refuted any propaganda that we members of the WAC had surrendered our femininity. We then removed the fancy objects and carefully replaced them with our military hats which we very proudly wore.

In this second month of the year there were vibrations of concern from home because my brother Leonard had communicated his unrest based on rumors that his company might be on the move. I heard from him too, although his letter to me discussed more personal thoughts since we both tempered our worries when writing to the next of kin. I explained to the family the system of Army gossip that was based on truth or no truth, and then hoped for the best.

I also received a snapshot of my sister Erma and her husband, Myron, who had been on leave from the Navy shortly before, and realized how precious a photograph could be. We girls had so many requests for them from family and friends, that I had photos of myself printed several at a time. I found a set of paints for portrait tinting so that the pictures I mailed to all and sundry were in color, which one hoped, added some zest to the viewing.

❦

At our own location, preparations to honor Valentine's Day were taking place, namely a show, in the form of a variety revue.

Public Relations Officer Lieutenant Gertrude Middleton appeared, and we two, with a crew, worked on skits, dance and song numbers while I, in addition, put up a background of decorations for the holiday that served, with embellishments, as the backdrop for the entertainment. I started with a giant red cardboard heart outlined in ruffled lace, then enlarged the theme to encompass a whole wall. For the dance numbers, our fatigue dresses were shortened to hip length and appropriate headpieces were created. An assortment of talents turned up amongst us, that had, until this time, lain dormant for purposes of the War. These now surfaced, and as they came into play, I designed, cut and stitched until all members were costumed and ready.

A Lieutenant at the Port area called to say that he had been in vaudeville and could he work with me. That was how Oscar Dvoretz and I became a team, and performed several song and dance routines which were broadly comedic, and paired us perfectly since we were both trained dancers with a flair for burlesque.

Our audience consisted of our Detachment with their invited guests and scores of uninvited visitors who arrived as the news spread. On the evening of the show, space was at such a premium that anything available for seating was placed everywhere and spilled over to the Mess Hall service area!

The cast was assembled, the band tuned up, we were primed and ready to go! How could we miss!—we didn't— we were a novelty and a "smash"—that left us all with a triumphant intoxicating headiness!

Up to this point there had been no attempt to do a WAC production within range of our location or one that was conceived by the military with only Armed Forces participants. We had requests to enlarge the revue and take it on the road but regulations did not allow such activity, therefore we had to be content with our success. Mission accomplished—we were a radiant and satisfied troupe!

❧

Now able to relax, I planned for my furlough to commence on March 15th, worked diligently in my office at my maps and drafting, took my turns at KP and other Detachment duties. I attended a performance of the Ballet Theater whose ranks had been depleted, like everyone else's due to the hostilities, and alerted my family to the fact that I would soon be home.

This leisurely cycle lasted very few days before a notice on the bulletin board summoned me to the office where I faced my Commanding Officer. The conversation sounded about like this:

Captain P.: "We have a recruitment drive starting, and have special work for you to do."

Me: "Ma'am, I am due for a furlough in a few weeks. I am exhausted as I have been doing two jobs and can use the rest."

Captain P.: "You will have to delay your vacation."

Me: "Then you are ordering me to do this job?"

Captain P.: "I am. We will set up an office for you here and we will supply you with everything you need."

Me: (reluctantly) "Yes, Ma'am!"

Captain P.:"You can have a three-day pass to any place you would like to go. You should be fresh and ready to start on Monday."

I accepted the pass, saluted, made the proper turn and left to pack! . . . Didn't I say we were there to serve?

❧

My office was organized in partnership with a WAC officer, Lieutenant Bloom, a reporter by trade, who was to act as liaison for newspaper and other publicity while I planned the displays, posters, illustrations and other workable forms of advertising to bring in the recruits. The Lieutenant and I set up our operation.

The room in the hotel assigned to us became an art center and a hatching nest for my conceptions. From this aerie originated three posters which were reproduced by the dozen to be placed around Seattle, and later were carried by our recruiting tour and placed in other cities in the state of Washington. In that office too, Lieutenant Bloom and I devised the idea of a climactic finale in the form of a Women's Army Corps parade—a demonstration of female military might!

One of my posters was on the idea of "Can You Refuse! Our Men Need Equipment—the Army Needs You!" It featured a photo of a WAC with our ship's-wheel shoulder insignia on her uniform. Another was informational and indicated the jobs we offered, recruitment locations, and choices of duty in the volunteer's home city. On a third, I used the catch phrase, "Let's Deliver the Goods," illustrated with a steamer and an airplane on their way—which was the work of the Transportation Corps. This became the theme adopted from my poster by the General in command of the Port area in his interviews and speeches during the recruitment campaign. In addition, it was the motto used on the banners in the WAC DAY presentation that concluded our enlistment efforts.

When I commenced my part of the project, I was authorized to utilize any departments necessary to accomplish the purpose. Permission was given to me for free access to the Motor Pool and the services of a Jeep and driver. I took advantage of the above while in search of supplies, for conferences with newspaper and Army people, and the distribution of material along with the numerous reproduction chores.

The sign shop at the Port had limited capacity to turn out certain portions of my work, therefore when all military means were exhausted, I enlisted the aid of an advertising firm whose name I selected from the telephone book.

The owner donated his time and facilities to instruct me in the silk-screen method, which accomplished the color process that the Army equipment could not.

All went well until the gentleman reasoned that since he was making his contribution to the War effort, the Women's Army Corps should be doing the same for him in return. On each of my visits, he flirted diligently while I flitted about the shop seeing to my posters and smiling pleasantly as I avoided the attempted clinches. When my work was completed, I loaded my Jeep for the last time, unknown to him, then amiably and winsomely backed out the door and made my escape before he endeavored another embrace!

War is Hell!

❦

The assignment also involved sketches for newspaper articles that appeared in the *Seattle Star* to accompany the account of our life style, written by a lady reporter who came to live with us for that purpose. These depicted the unique type of decoration in our hotel rooms such as our petite Mess Sergeant butchering an enormous side of beef, the new automatic potato peeler bouncing the spuds around while a KP was enjoying her ease and also a fun time pursuit, our Ouija board, the Company prognosticator, in action.

From my office too, emanated the drawings that accompanied other phases in the activities of our Corps for additional news stories, recruiting pamphlets and bulletins, and from the same source came illustrations for handouts placed at stores and other public places. Some of these items contained written materials of my own, others by Lieutenant Bloom or the Recruiting office. For weeks we did the preparatory work until the drive was officially made public.

The art part of the project was of a home-grown variety.

After I had devised the ideas, made the samples, cajoled various departments into providing materials and services—I did some or all of the printing and distributed the displays. There were no "hours." "'Round the clock" and "double-time" were the order of the day in this War period. When I would forget to attend mess, some friendly head appeared in the door with a reminder. My compatriots were aware of the fact that I did not always remember to eat! Even after adequate meals, late night work made me a candidate for quick energy lifts, to which end there was a steady supply of chocolate bars.

ॐ

To open our campaign, the Frederick & Nelson department store dressed one of its windows in the furnishings of our WAC quarters and used one of my recruiting posters to emphasize the purpose of our drive. Advertisements appeared (again Frederick & Nelson's), for a fashion parade to be held daily, for which I was asked to be the commentator.

Our officers arranged for the review and asked local and distant Quartermaster Departments for a sampling of all female clothing with accessories, as used in Service. A complete wardrobe was assembled, and our girls showed the outfits of commissioned and enlisted women. They wore clothes used stateside, overseas and at distant stations that called for unique creations; there were also on-duty, off-duty items, various dress costumes and the uniforms of the Nursing Corps and hospital attendants. Presented too was snow-wear for the far north as well as tropic suits with safari hats worn in the jungle. In addition, we had appropriate footwear, head coverings, sleeping wardrobes, lingerie, and outfits for uncommon jobs, and even gear worn at the fighting fronts with helmets and pack equipment.

In my case, the fashion promenade meant that I dropped

any project at hand, whether in or out of the hotel, changed to a fresh dress uniform, then dashed to the department store and stepped from the wings onto the auditorium stage to deliver the commentary, while my friends modeled.

I and my officers appeared at motion picture houses between shows, where we made our pitches for recruitment. We extended an invitation for the public to "come one and all" to visit with us in our hotel quarters. We threw open our doors one evening, a week before the peak of the campaign, and men, women and children streamed in. They were welcomed from below the street level to the rafters where they viewed our military home and asked questions.

"Where and how do you eat?"

"In the Mess Hall, in cafeteria style!"

"Do the cooks really handle that giant equipment?"

"They sure do!"

"Who washes those big pots?"

"We do, Mam!" "Cots, green blankets and footlockers— why not hotel beds?"

"We're in the Army now!"

"Do you do your own laundry? Who cleans the hotel? Who runs the elevator?"

"We, we, we—we are the laundresses, the house cleaners, the elevator operators—in addition, we are the scullery maids, and charwomen!"

This open house was one way to bring people closer to the ladies of the Corps and to clarify the mystery of who we were and how we functioned. There were curiosities to be satisfied about our transition from civilians to female soldiers in wartime.

❦

We worked long hours on the publicity campaign, thus on two occasions, our small group, which consisted of me, male and female co-workers and Lieutenant Bloom, went to the local USO for an ice cream treat, relaxation, and shop talk. Lieutenant Bloom, a commissioned officer, in the Enlisted Men's Club? You bet! She, being of a daintier build than the rest of us, was placed in the center as we surrounded her, walked through the door and up the stairs where we settled in a secluded corner. Later, after sodas, sundaes and chatter, we exited the same way.

❦

Plans continued for an aforementioned display to cap the WAC week recruitment. In the interest of this project, Lieutenant Bloom and I, and my Commanding Officer again appealed to the Commandants of distant Armed Forces bases as well as our own, to send military hardware. All WAC personnel from surrounding areas that could be spared, would be included. Posts, Stations, Bases and Forts responded to our requests, and promised to supply whatever ladies and equipment they could.

When the day dawned, and the forces were assembled, we were overwhelmed with the size and scope of the turnout!

We had bombarded the town for weeks, and this was the result of our efforts! It included companies of our ladies marching in full battle dress with guns and gunnery paraphernalia, and motorized troops in tanks, trucks and jeeps all driven by members of the Women's Army Corps. Banners covered the hardware, and flags flew from each marching unit. The WAC Band came from Des Moines, Iowa, and the rest of the participants were those from Fort Lewis, Fort Lawton, my own detachment at the Seattle Port of Embarkation and surrounding air bases. The only servicemen were musicians stationed at the Port and Lawton. It was impressive! We hoped the result would be an enormous enrollment of women, for that was what we needed and had worked for.

Ceremonies included speeches by Army dignitaries, and the spectacle culminated in a swearing-in of four recruits for purposes of publicity, with more to follow them by way of regular enlistment proceedings.

I rode in a Jeep at the rear of the procession, very tired, and enormously grateful for the results of our combined efforts and the cooperation of those with whom we had toiled.

☙

The effort in Seattle was finished, but our work in that direction had not been completed. Several days prior, I had received notice that eight service people, including me, were to tour several towns in Washington for eight days and bring our message to "Deliver the Goods!" Our destinations were Tacoma, Olympia, Centralia, Chekalis, Raymond, Aberdeen and Hoquiam, in western Washington state.

The team consisted of a WAC Captain who was a recruiter, Lieutenant Bloom handling the publicity, and three enlisted women of which I was one, who represented the Service, Ground and Air Forces. With us were three men; our photographer, Sergeant Richmond, and two chauffeurs for the vehicles—a travel van and a sedan. The men slept in the van each night while we ladies took advantage of the local hotel facilities.

We moved in two sections; our advance group in the car carried a supply of my fliers and posters; and when we arrived in town, we immediately contacted the radio stations for interviews, the high schools for the use of their bands, the motion picture houses and the newspapers—all for promotion purposes. I went to the stations to broadcast with a staff member and if there was not any available, I did a commercial blurb on behalf of our procurement efforts, entreated the public to view a small parade (the high school band with our banners and posters exhibited), and reminded them to come to our mobile office the next day for information. In the meantime, Lieutenant Bloom took her news releases to the local papers while the other women placed posters in store windows, fliers on the counters and manned the enrollment desk in our travel vehicle.

We also visited the Mayors' offices and the Fire and Police Departments to get permission for our equipment which sometimes blocked traffic. The Fire Chiefs and Chiefs of Police invariably asked us to look over their facilities where pictures were taken with them and appeared in the newspapers the day after with our recruiting notices. During this circuit, we were invited to have our photos taken at the Police Headquarters in Aberdeen. These were "mug shots" taken by the Chief himself who was rightly proud of his latest laboratory equipment; and to our surprise, were the finest service portraits we each had had up to that time.

In the evening, one or two of us went to the theaters to speak to the audiences, plead our cause, detail our style of life, Military pay and benefits such as medical care, types and places of employment, and the several services to choose from.

The second half of our contingent, the WAC Captain, our photographer and the alternate chauffeur arrived the following day in the Silver Air Stream which was equipped for enlistment. The high school band attracted attention to our location where we always hoped for a good turnout of volunteers.

People were cordial and kind to us in each town, for which we were grateful. In Centralia, Washington, always pressed for time, I washed and set my hair, and in the absence of a dryer was generously invited to use one at a beauty salon near our hotel with the warm comment, ". . . just remember that a lady in Centralia invited you to use her facilities when in need of them" . . . and I have.

During the frantic eight-day campaign, I wrote home to say that I had done everything but a fan dance, my impersonation of Mrs. Roosevelt and a buck and wing tap number.

❦

Back at the Hotel Stratford after the whirlwind jaunt, I, with a group of others, found that we had been awarded the Good Conduct Medal for "honorable and faithful service and excellent character." On the wings of those gracious words I at last packed for my furlough.

When I entered the coach I was dressed in my vacation wardrobe of olive drabs with accessories and I again carried my modest piece of luggage, A miniature barracks bag held my cosmetics and etceteras and since that tiny bag was novel, and I had not seen another like it, I had developed a fondness for it. Apparently it was highly thought of by some admiring stranger who stole it with all its contents, while I freshened myself in a station restroom! The risks of War!

Like my previous experience crossing the country for four days, this too was broadening and enlightening. Many of the civilian passengers were attentive to me, wished to know what they could do to make life better for other GIs or how to best help their own loved ones. When my advice and counsel were sought, I replied to the best of my knowledge.

We hummed along toward the East, made the appointed station stops during which cars were sometimes detached and recoupled or crews rotated. At such intervals, before the aforementioned changeovers, we usually stepped out of the train, stretched our legs, inhaled some fresh air, and then at the sound of the "All aboard," reembarked for the continued journey. At Harrisburg, Pennsylvania, several of us stood and chatted while the rolling stock boomed and tooted its way to the far end of the station and back several times in the process of rearranging its cars. Another soldier and I, deep in conversation, awaited that familiar call from the conductor. The train geared up and hooted its way to the far end of the station once more, and while we all gazed in stunned amazement, continued its rhythmical grind as it slowly faded into the distance! There had been no "All aboard"; at least not where it could be heard by us, and there we stood—stranded!

Does one laugh or cry?! We decided to laugh!—then hurried into the station and utilized the services of the nearest Army depot and the railroad company, whose employees wired ahead to have our belongings, which were stowed in the moving vehicle, held for us at our ultimate point of destination.

Sergeant Lew Schwartz and I, now compatriots in an adventure, telephoned relatives, found sleeping places for the night with the assistance of Military authorities, and in the morning claimed our waiting luggage at Penn Station in New York.

Can this happen twice? Well in a way it did—for in my first "Dear folks" letter of March 13, 1943, written on the initial trip to Basic Training, I related to my family that a porter offered to mail our postcards, and alas, he too was left behind in fateful Harrisburg!

"All's well that ends well!" We were each at home again!

My brother Leonard rushed from Fort Eustis, Virginia, to Brooklyn for a reunion. It was his first glimpse of me in uniform and my first sight of him in his military state. We were overjoyed with the meeting and so proud of one another. For the occasion he arrived in a handsome dress outfit.

ॐ

While on vacation, I kept my promise to visit with my former Commanding Officer, Ida Stoller, who was at Fort Hamilton, Brooklyn. She confirmed the rumor that her change of station had been maneuvered by an upper echelon of WAC officers and that Wilhelmina Hinton, who had been her second in command and was still with our company, would be the next target for reassignment. Lieutenant Hinton's replacement would round out the coterie now composed of our current Commander and her allies at the Port of Embarkation office.

Ida Stoller, devoted to those who attended their jobs conscientiously, sought my assistance in rallying the noncommissioned personnel to indicate to the Port Commander our esteem for her former aide's performance of her duties. Should an attempt be made to place the Lieutenant in an unfavorable position, our efforts on her behalf would instead reflect her integrity and devotion to the principles of the Women's Army Corps.

On my return, I visited with several of our women, who, aware of the situation, pledged their cooperation—but the utilization of their offers was not a simple matter. Lieutenant Hinton felt it best that we not speak for her fearing the consequences for all, and remained resolute in her determination to endure the situation as an officer and a lady. She was replaced shortly afterward!

This completed the clique and reflected the change in the total slate of company and POE officers, whereon we, who had sworn obedience to the greater good, adjusted ourselves to the requirements of these successors.

❦

After my furlough, I rejoined my Company but not my partner at the Drafting and Blueprint office because another soldier had temporarily replaced me until a permanent place could be found for him elsewhere. I spent this time at general office duties at the Port Engineer's Department and was ultimately returned to my own drawing board.

Employment in the Army was not of our own choosing, but made to meet the needs of the Military. We performed any tasks that we were ordered to do. If we wished, we could apply for assignment changes with no guarantee that our requests would be granted. Sometimes, fortunately, we were authorized to the preferred position.

When I was resettled in my office, it seemed opportune to inquire of the Captain in charge of my department at the harbor area, why I had not received a promotion. I felt that he had bypassed me without due cause, that I had worked faithfully and diligently at two jobs, one at the Port and the other, at my headquarters, and that I had been a "professional" Private First Class long enough. With the agreement, urging and encouragement of my fellow soldiers in the Blueprint section, I braced myself to "ask the Boss for a raise!"

I stated my case to Captain Nelson, my superior officer. He was silent for a moment, then showed me my file with his complimentary rating of my work and personal conduct. He told me that I had twice been recommended by him for raises in grade, subject to the approval of the Commanding Officer of the WAC at the Port, and the head of my own detachment. These requests had been denied each time at both levels! What had I done wrong!

The Captain was irate on my behalf and told me that I would have to contend with the jealousy of the WAC officers and recommended that I "look in the mirror, girl!" I blushed furiously since I was dreadfully shy, nettled by the inference in the statement, the denial of my promotion, and his suggestion as to the cause. He considerately helped a modest young lady realize that the human element was present in the Women's Army Corps. Later I was most grateful for his words that served to enhance my awareness and assist in the process of my maturity.

NEW FIELDS VIA
THE CIRCUITOUS ROUTE

Under the circumstances of my discussion with Captain Nelson I felt that I had given my best to the successful completion of a huge task and would like to continue my work, but not assume a job in a thankless situation. Toil itself I would never shun and there was still a War out there to be reckoned with and a choice of locations from which to place my ammunition and take my best shot. I requested, and was granted, a transfer to the environs of New Orleans, Louisiana. When the travel orders were printed, I was fortunate to have been allowed a few extra days to stop at Fort Smith, Arkansas, to visit with my current heart interest, Danny, so in early July I started out.

When soldiers change location they carry their entire possessions with them which means wardrobe, and other personal articles, therefore one need learn to live and pack thriftily. We were issued two barracks bags (or duffels) for this purpose and that is how we moved—the bags took the place of many pieces of luggage. When on a lone trip, I used one of these canvas bags and a valise since two of them would have been awkward to transport. En route from one place to another, a male soldier usually alleviated the struggle with this cargo by swinging my duffel over one shoulder even if he had his own on the other. We enjoyed the compatriotic privileges and the closeness of soldiers in wartime.

It was during this change of posts that I had the unique

experience of riding into Fort Smith on a train which might have been taken out of a railroad museum and pressed into service in the expediency of getting on with the War and the resultant shortages of transportation. The seats were upholstered in caning and framed in wood, a form of construction of a bygone era, and the sides, open to the floor, were windowless and exposed to the elements. This should have allowed any currents that might be available, to course through, but there weren't any breezes in the stifling heat of that early July. What we lacked in the gracious qualities of soothing drafts was abetted by the quantities of soot thrown up by the action of the wheels and the smoke from the engine. This combination of grit and dust came in through the unshielded sides of the cars and made a very grimy journey. There was a primitively equipped restroom sans a sink, to accommodate the demands of our needs, which it barely accomplished.

This may have been the original train used by the Union Pacific Line to open the way to the West in the great expansion of the 19th century. When I gazed down in the direction of my dirty lap and at the condition of my fellow passengers, I was surprised to see that our costumes were out of keeping with the period of the vehicle; that we ladies were not in bustles nor the men in cutaway coats with high silk hats. . . ! The state of my person in Fort Smith, cinders and all, took second place to the happy reunion only two soldiers can know in a precarious epoch. I then wended my way to my new post in New Orleans, Louisiana, and reached there the 7th of July, 1944.

One of the officers formerly at the Seattle Port of Embarkation was now at Camp Plauché, Louisiana, and I looked forward to seeing Lieutenant Gertrude Middleton (now Spear) with whom I had joined forces for the Valentine's Day Show in Seattle. She received me with warmth and after a quick exchange of news, told me to "Get out quick, this is a mud hole" which would provide no opportunity for me to make a meaningful contribution in the Public Relations and Special Services activities we were both familiar with whereon I bowed to her good judgement. She then arranged for me to be transferred across town to the Transportation Corps School on Lake Ponchartrain—under the command of Lieutenant Marjorie Marriage.

ื

Since my arrival and reassignment were completed all in one day, I moved from the devilish mire of Plauché to the cement streets of the new post, where I seemed to have walked into Heaven—for as the First Sergeant opened the barracks' door, clouds of ethereal gauze floated in the mist! Was it truly Elysium? — No! — Only waves of white mosquito netting atop every cot to prevent Uncle Sam's girls from being bitten above and beyond the call of duty in the tropical climate.

Changes occurred swiftly in our capacities as soldiers, where acclimating need be instantaneous, so, after a few gulps of the celestial sight, I unpacked my things at my designated space, inquired about my new job, met my superior officer, acquainted myself with the immediate WAC area, and made myself "at home away from home."

My title and address became:

P.F.C. Clarice M. Fortgang
Headquarters and Headquarters Detachment
Transportation Corps School
New Orleans Army Air Base
New Orleans 12, Louisiana

Later in the evening, when my fellow volunteers and I prepared for bed, we draped the billows of netting about our cots and were off to sleep.

The crack of dawn brought a rude awakening, an invasion? — ! From the outside I heard the shouts of male voices, clear and unclear! "Come on men," banging, shots, more voices and "walkie talkies," surrounded the building.

The thudding sounds of bodies, the scraping and grating of equipment outside, and God! — yes! — even underneath the floor, as grunts, rustling, and shots continued to ring out!

I froze and my heart thumped wildly! Shortly afterward, I heard the others stirring, groaning, and complaining volubly as they awakened. "Damn" — !

It seemed that we were in the line of fire for the Obstacle Course practice which took place several days a week. That particular training took the troops under and around the WAC encampment, which made for a shortened rest on such occasions! But then, didn't everybody have an Obstacle Course running through their barracks? We thought they did!

❦

One moved slowly in the moist atmosphere of New Orleans and the Transportation Corps Base with advice offered from barracks mates about how to accustom oneself to the climate. It included the fact that three weeks was required to function at a productive level in the heat and humidity, and salt tablets were the recommendation. The ones supplied by the Medical Department were not to my taste and rejected by my physical system; an additional amount on my food seemed to be more agreeable. Lieutenant Marriage kept on an even keel by sipping her ever-present glass of saline solution at intervals throughout the day.

❦

The focus in Detachment life and duty requirements here was at variance with that of Seattle where the spectrum of WAC occupations ran the gamut. At that port, several of our enlisted women were in full charge of the offices that fed, clothed and armed our men. Then there were jobs such as the one I had recently left in the Drafting and Blueprint Section that kept charts of troops and matériel up to the minute and also the women employed in Quartermaster who received all incoming goods necessary to fight the War, then saw to it that those same armaments, large and small, were placed aboard ships and sent on their way. Our ladies in Seattle broadened their spheres of operation every day when they extended their skills beyond their original assignments.

The field of view at Lake Ponchartrain was narrower, with the main complement of the Corps concerned with necessary tasks on the post without the wide scope of abilities required at a bustling port. The needs here, less diverse, largely attracted WAC members to fit that bill. At the close of a work day, personal choices for relaxation differed in kind at this location too, where downing a mug of good cheer appeared to be the preferred pastime.

❦

I was now engaged at clerking duties for which I had been trained in Texas. This placed me in a routine but pleasant atmosphere, and after hours, allowed time to visit the French Quarter and Vieux Carré (Old Square) by way of the "Desire" streetcar that stopped outside our base.

When I boarded the trolley on my first reconnaissance into the city, it was abruptly brought to mind that I was below the Mason-Dixon line. The very idea that I was not expected to move to the back of the car if it became crowded, was a thought foreign to me. I debated this as I was edged along by other passengers and decided to move to the rear of the vehicle when necessary, and let the immediate need take care of the situation. I encountered puzzled looks and stares, friendly and otherwise, stood where I felt appropriate, and then exited at my destination. Later trips were made in the company of other soldiers, in which case we moved or sat where space and fitness dictated.

❦

This new station had taken on a friendly note for me not long before I came there because Mother's youngest brother, Captain Mack Kittay, had recently married in New Orleans. My aunt, nee Fannie Dennery, and her relatives were old inhabitants of Louisiana and interested in their own history, so tales and tours of the ancient city were a part of our hours spent together.

Since my evenings were free, I joined the New Orleans Opera Association chorus and found myself in rehearsal for *Aida*, under the direction of Maestro Walter Herbert. Just before the performance on November 2, however, my furlough time came due, and aware that these vacation schedules could be uncertain, I took advantage of mine and went home. This was the first time in my theatrical life (which commenced at the age of five), that I did not carry through a performance from practice to the opening night curtain! The "ham" in me was left unfulfilled!

This had to be War!

❦

After I had settled in, my record was reviewed by my Commanding Officer and showed "Entertainment Specialist" to be one of my occupations, I was again drafted for extra duty because there was a definite need to enliven the leisure hours in our own WAC barracks. Since recreational activities were left to the individual women, very little took place. Lieutenant Marriage was enthusiastic about my plan to have a get-together for the girls of the

Detachment and the Officer Candidates of the Transportation Corps School, who, during the first few weeks of their studies, were restricted to the base. This idea had not been used before and the approach seemed novel and refreshing. On behalf of my company, I delivered a tongue-in-cheek request for the present class to be our guests at a Garden Party in their honor, and asked, due to the exigencies of the War, that they please forego the "White Tie and Tails!"

In the same spirit the Candidate Company Commander sent the following reply:

OFFICER CANDIDATE CLASS #29
TRANSPORTATION CORPS SCHOOL
NEW ORLEANS ARMY AIR BASE
New Orleans 12, Louisiana

HM/sl
11 August 1944

Subject: Acknowledgement of Invitation.
To: Members, Hq & Hq Det, WAC,
             NOAAB, New Orleans 12, La.

1. Receipt is acknowledged of your invitation to attend a dance and garden party in honor of the Officer Candidates of Class 29.

2. The members of the class happily accept this invitation and will attend en masse.

3. In compliance with your request no class member will appear in "tails."

4. The class wishes to thank you for your thoughtfulness in extending this courtesy.

LARRY MELMAN
Cand. Co. Comdr.,
OCS Class 29
Trans Corps School

We readied ourselves with Chinese lanterns and any other colorful decorating goods we could find and arranged to have a platform set up for dancing—even our cooks were inspired to create an original buffet. The overall effect was a contrast to the yards of olive drabness and the standard white buildings.

Our guests approached the party site at the appointed hour polished, pressed, marching in unison and singing a song of serenade. At the words of command—"Company halt—break ranks," they did, and the festivities began, albeit with a reduced number of women. Alas, some had abandoned our fun evening to sip beer in town.

The soon-to-be-officers expressed their pleasure with our efforts, while we all made merry until the wee hours.

❦

The radio station located in the St. Charles Hotel in New Orleans devoted an evening a week to the Armed Forces. The programs featured personal profiles of people in the Services but was short of news from any females. The Public Relations department sent inquiries to our Detachment about whom they could present, and our Company officer recommended an interview with me. Afterward the station staff asked that I locate other conversational or entertainment possibilities, so to this end, I scouted the men and women and discovered singers, instrumentalists and other talents on the base.

Front and Back of the Barbed Wire

We had invited our fellow American servicemen to a party in the hope of alleviating the strains of the blitz courses they were involved in and the uncertainty of where they would go next. My phalanx of ladies, too, needed relief from their unceasing work and the humid weather—but what of the enemy who had created the necessity for this immense gathering of men, women, and matériel in this gargantuan effort! Where were they?

The foes were not only in the faraway reaches of the world, but were also on our shores—and furthermore—they were on the grounds of the Transportation Corps School! We were sharing our military space with prisoners of war from Italy and Germany!

During my time spent in association with the WAC Headquarters, I had occasion to visit the Public Relations Office at a distant corner of the post where the German prisoners were confined. They were billeted in buildings behind barbed wire fences and their lot was not a happy one. They were outdoors on a daily basis, where they painted and repaired their own quarters. When I walked by I was treated to dour expressions on the part of some and the same expression combined with curiosity on the part of others. Heavily guarded, there was never a pause in the bang, bang of the hammers or a hesitation in the slap, slap of the paint brushes and the scraping of the ladders being moved.

The policy toward the internment of the Italian prisoners differed, since some were assigned duties in our offices and about the grounds where they were employed in keeping them neat. A reserved but friendly smile and a special look, was forthcoming from them to let each woman know she was appreciated as a "female" female.

One Italian prisoner at work in another department whom I saw several times while on detachment business, showed me a watercolor study he had made in Oran, Algeria, before he was captured in North Africa. I spoke a minim of Italian and he no English, but each understood the other to be an artist, which we expressed in broken bits of one another's language while we flung our hands to and fro. He eventually bestowed on me as a gift of friendship the only item of value he possessed, that painting done in Oran. I hung this in our Day Room fully appreciative of the heartwarming exchange of amity encompassed in this offering.

'Meet The Public'

There were excursions out of the office, but most of my time was spent inside, assisting in accumulating and processing the day's records, and other business of running the Headquarters.

One afternoon, several weeks after I joined the company, I was alone at the Detachment, when a high-ranking officer, who was expected for an inspection tour, arrived, accompanied by her retinue. While we awaited the return of Lieutenant Marriage, the visitor suggested that I escort their party through all barracks, Day Room and general areas during which time they inquired into working conditions and the morale of the unit. I answered their queries to the best of my knowledge and since my Company Commander still had not returned by the completion of our rounds, the officers indicated that they could wait no longer, declined refreshments, offered their regrets and took their leave.

A few weeks later, my Lieutenant received a letter from the center of operations of the Women's Army Corps advising her that I would be more effective if I represented the WAC in some capacity where I came in contact with the civilian populace. Shortly afterward orders came through for me to report for recruiting duty in New Orleans proper, "to meet the Public!"

Motor Pool took me into town with my valise and barracks bags, where I found a comfortable place to live in the home of a lady who had several rooms to let. She was accustomed to having a daughter about, (hers being elsewhere at the time) and made me feel at home to the extent of preparing chicory coffee for me in the morning in Louisiana style, for which I had not as yet developed a taste. I was graciously invited to use the kitchen facilities, and to relax in her living room.

This was also my first contact with those early settlers in the South, cockroaches—which abounded throughout the apartment and with which my landlady had a long and intimate relationship. The philosophy of live and let live extended to the interior of the refrigerator where the roaches were given free rein. Offers to share breakfast in the morning with this kindly woman were proffered regularly, but any inclination I might have had to accept, were curbed by the thought of involvement with the inside of the refrigerator.

When we became better known to one another, my hostess brought forth from its resting place a box of memories. It contained old opera and concert programs, long white kid gloves, a fan, visiting cards and photographs of known concert performers of an earlier era. She told me her father, Louis P. Verande, had been an impresario. The stars who arrived to perform their roles at the French Opera House or to sing or play in concert, were entertained in her girlhood home and she had attended every performance with her family—long since gone.

At a later date, when space became available, I suggested to two male soldiers on detached duty in town, that her rooms would be comfortable for them too, so, during the evenings we had a companionable group of GIs. We were located near City Park in New Orleans, spent pleasant after-hours at dinner, and then strolled amidst the greenery and flowers which made our jobs in the city of New Orleans less stark for all of us.

This new job bore no resemblance to my creative effort at the Seattle Port of Embarkation, for here it consisted of my assignment as a lone soldier representing the WAC. Desk space was provided for me on the main thoroughfare, Canal Street, opposite the French Quarter in a booth where War Bonds were sold.

During my work day I was not the sole tenant in the Recruiting Booth. The other occupant was a gracious lady, Amelia Sentilles, who sold the Bonds and took a personal interest in me and whose daughter, Ethel, was in the Women's Army too, on assignment elsewhere. Mrs. Sentilles, whom I called "Mom" kept watch on my side of the room while she attended to bond sales. Since we were centrally located, we not only dispensed information about the city and the WAC, but were a meeting place for members of the Armed Services who were off duty, between stations or on furlough and wanted to while away the time in the company of Mom and me who represented mother, wife, sweetheart and sister.

Mom approved or disapproved of the men who paid close attention to me in her own particular way. If they met with her favor (I had only to glance in her direction to find out) she smiled to indicate a complimentary opinion—if not, there was a censoring frown or in the extreme, a flashing distress signal. She explained apologetically that she was as caring about the male company I chose as she might be on behalf of any member of her own family.

Her concern for my welfare was returned by my affection for her.

She and her husband, Charles Sentilles, "Dad," were like a second set of parents in their consideration for me, and much of my off- duty time was spent in their company eating fried chicken and touring places of interest.

❧

During the hottest season, before I moved into town, there was an advantage in being attached to the company at Lake Ponchartrain because we adjoined a public beach, and even though we were just next door, we had to take a bus to the outside of the Base and change trolleys to get back to the bordering shore.

On dates, it was cool and picturesque to take an evening

sail on the Mississippi, where we could dine and dance aboard the cruise steamers. I also loved to be down along the river where seafood delights were served such as a tray of steamed crabs and shrimp accompanied by miniature pretzels and pitchers of cold beer. The appetite was whetted at the entrance to Brunings restaurant because the fishnets that dawdled and drifted in the water to gather the shellfish, were hung from the railings at each side of the plank walk that led to the front door. When orders were taken, the nets were raised and the contents steamed and served in record time. Although the trays of food always looked like "too much," we invariably met the challenge and did the Army proud by leaving nary a crumb.

In town, St. Phillip Street in the French Quarter harbored a cozy hidden store. The proprietor, a religious man, prepared Italian style sandwiches, where the choice of sizes was large, larger and huge. The "large" was the small size and was generous enough for two adequate meals.

The shop was lit with a dim bulb, which glow was enhanced by rows of shelves lined with religious pictures and candles aglow day and night. The sandwich ingredients were arrayed in front of the proprietor who genially inquired what size roll you preferred to house the delights he was prepared to set onto it, then the procedure began. Between the talk of the day interspersed with blessings, he moved from platter to platter and bowl to bowl heaping on meats, cheeses and trimmings; even when it seemed the tower would surely topple, more was piled on.

One viewed the building of this edifice with an eye to delighting the taste buds and giving the jaws and teeth some exercise, with the consideration of how wide the mouth could open to encompass the anticipated gustatory wonder. It never could expand enough—with the result that each "bite" had to be done in two or three bites. Visitors received a blessing and "Bon Appetito" on departure and then with the heavenly odors tantalizing the senses, one repaired to the nearest haven to tear open the food-stained wrapping and to contemplate how best to approach the oversized treat—from the bottom, the top or the middle!

If all else failed to entertain, there was always the Tea Parlor and one could have tea leaves read—with sometimes curious results. The lady who read mine told me that I would meet two men, one dark haired and one blond, and that both would ask me out and I would accept a date with the dark-haired man. A day or two later while Mrs. Sentilles and I were in the recruiting booth, two Naval officers entered, one dark haired and one blond. Mom signaled with her eyes and I made a choice in accord with hers. When asked for dates by both men—it seemed more appropriate to accept one with the dark-haired one—she smiled in agreement. The lady of the tea leaves also foretold of an association with a "white-haired man with green eyes—not old, but white haired." A few days later the Public Relations officer, Lieutenant Boykin, who sent for me to speak at a meeting of the Girl Scouts, had white hair and green eyes! Also at the time of my tenure in town, the Maison Blanche department store generously offered a free sitting and photograph to all Service personnel. I took advantage of this gift and the store mailed them to whomever we wished. I have been forever grateful to them.

New orders lengthened my recruiting activities into December. Highlights during my tour of duty in New Orleans were visits from my father and brother Leonard. Daddy, who would find his way through war and peace to get to us, found his way to New Orleans, which extended his present cotton-buying trip by many miles. This was a great treat for us both because I could show him the colorful and historic city and we could indulge in some of the renowned food within the limits of availability in wartime.

My brother, who was enroute from his assignment in Georgia to another post in San Antonio, Texas, traveled by way of New Orleans so that we two could have a reunion. I met him and his friend at the train station at midnight and we were all together until 4 in the morning. This precious time was spent at the Hotel Roosevelt on Canal Street where we ate, danced and I sang with the band. It was a memorable evening. These treasured hours with Leonard and my father were as close as I could get then to a family reunion.

Strange Bedfellows
and New School Ways

I was eventually granted a furlough. Armed with that happy fact, I wended my way home to Brooklyn, New York. Twasn't easy!

By Army rumor antenna, I received information that since the Base on Lake Ponchartrain adjoined Naval and Coast Guard stations, one could appear at the Naval Airport, and if a plane was going one's way, one could "hitch a ride" and save the travel time on a train—and some money too!

How appealing!

I called and was told to be at the Airport by 8:00 P.M. and I was. I was also there at 10:30, —11:00, and 12:30 A.M.—having received several notices through the evening that the plane would be in "shortly."

A Coast Guard Officer appeared bound for Baltimore, Maryland, and that made three of us, he and I and a dispatcher who sat in a cubicle apart from us in a dimly lit little room which was the Airport headquarters. Still later, another Officer of the Coast Guard, Lieutenant Ackerman, hurried in expectantly with his wife. Brooklyn was their destination too! We all speculated about the trip while we chatted hopefully. At long last, sometime in the night, we boarded an airplane with other passengers already settled in their places, and took off into the darkness. We held our breaths as we headed northeast since we couldn't believe we were on the way. I held not only my breath, but my hand over my mouth as well since the air pockets over Louisiana affected me adversely.

A whispered consultation started amongst the pilots and passengers; the upshot was that our group would be bumped from the plane in Atlanta, Georgia. The spaces were promised to higher-ranking personnel.

Now grounded at the airport, our two men went off and eventually reappeared with train accommodations, one coach seat and one roomette. It was decided that the Ackermans and I would share the roomette, and the unaccompanied officer use the coach, since he was not going as far as we.

While our friend found his way to his car, the Ackermans and I, bleary-eyed, repaired to our quarters. We agreed that I would have the upper and they the lower. The three of us, grateful for the prospect of a few hours sleep, collapsed into our bunks. At daybreak, we pulled into a station where I peeked through my window and saw our lone friend greeted affectionately by his wife and small child and then fell asleep again thankful for the mattress beneath me.

At the journey's end, I met my family and not only viewed the trials of the circuitous trip with humor but rediscovered how small was this world. It seemed that Lieutenant and Mrs. Ackerman were neighbors of family friends in Brooklyn, where the retelling of our tribulations led to the mention of my name and—voilà! everyone knew everyone else! These were sterling companions of the night, and for all of us it was "where there's a will, there's a way" and we had made it home. Warring indeed makes odd bedfellows!

❧

The return experience paled by comparison since it lacked such exotics as a flight by night and was accomplished by train. News awaited me on my arrival that the germ of an idea which had been planted months before, had taken root! The seed I had sown was an appeal for a change of occupation because the recruitment assignment in New Orleans did not need my "all" and did not satisfy the sensation of progress toward a successful conclusion of the War. Traditions that led to the reluctance of females to volunteer for the Women's Army at that time and place, were stumbling blocks in the path of the WAC.

From the 25th of August to the 9th of December, I had been on duty in town, then rejoined my company at the Detachment to prepare for my requested training at the Army School for Personnel Services in Lexington, Virginia. Of the variety of courses there, mine had to do with soldier shows which was one of the kinds of work I had already been involved in.

When the time came to leave, we were a party of five, three women and two servicemen who, armed with orders and meal coupons, boarded the train that would take us to Virginia—then with the familiar belching of the whistles, the slow grinding of the wheels and the lurching of the cars, we settled down to a steady pace and were on our way.

LEGITIMATE AT LAST!

Following our arrival at Washington and Lee University, now occupied by the Military, we were quartered in fraternity houses and dormitories on the campus. Thanks to a recent promotion all mail that came to me would now be addressed:

Corporal Clarice M. Fortgang
School for Personnel Services
Army Service Forces. Co. A. Class #28
Washington and Lee University
Lexington, Virginia

After our belongings were stowed and we had the leisure to gaze about, the scene that met our eyes was affecting. We took note of the properties of the pre-war occupants and the pieces of their lives they had left behind. Remnants of rock collections and other specimens stood on book shelves and window sills; notebooks, pens, pencils and personal items lay about dusty and abandoned. The point hit home that those who preceded the Army residents in these dormitories had forsaken these lodgings under the circumstances of the outbreak of hostilities. Classes were held in a number of buildings where more reminders of the late tenants could be seen and one could not help but feel their presences there.

❦

In contrast to its former atmosphere, the campus was now host to a teeming assemblage of male and female personnel, both commissioned and enlisted, who represented the four corners of the War. There was no segregation of rank amongst the soldiery congregated to imbibe the ways and means of recreational and educational morale building. I too had come a distance since the eighteen months or so previous, when Nacogdoches, Texas, was my sole experience at an Armed Forces school then restricted to the Women's Army Corps and its limited sphere of operations.

Here were the current stars in their own professions, now in the Service. The public relations and advertising businesses were represented, so were the acting, dancing, musical and costume designing professions, also people experienced in all forms of stagecraft, before and behind the footlights. There were those who were proficient in the business of military funding, production of Army entertainment, and the organization of recreational games. Others were there to teach procedures for discussion forums, school classes and the mental and physical reconditioning of the wounded.

After my extra-hour activities at the Seattle Port of Embarkation and the Transportation Corps School in New Orleans, I was finally allowed to be a Special Service person—legitimacy had come to me at last!

The level of excitement exhibited at the school infused those who passed through it with the energy to raise the esprit de corps of the many we were to serve throughout the Military. This was our assigned purpose. All schedules operated under six departments: Athletic and Recreation, Information and Education, Military Training, Operations, Personal Affairs and Reconditioning. There were 24 rooms used for lecture halls and classes—depending upon the subjects. Uniforms of various kinds were needed in six classifications from "dress" to "athletic."

My work, part of the Athletic and Recreation Course, dealt with the Production and Management of Soldier Shows under which was Program Planning, Handicrafts (which included costuming, wigs and scenery). There were general subject matters in which all departments participated such as: Administration, Funding, Organization, Military Correspondence, and Facilities. On the list, too, were Morale and Leadership, Personal Affairs, and Films. Our Army association was not forgotten, so physical conditioning was required, and we assembled for Battalion Inspection and Review by the Training Staff too.

The courses, as outlined, kept us busy from 8:00 in the morning to 5:30 in the afternoon, interrupted only by lunch and evening mess. After that there were meetings and briefings, practice scenes from plays or rehearsal for an extravaganza of a show that involved nearly all students in all departments of my curriculum either on the stage, in the orchestra or behind the scenes—until we fell into bed exhausted!

On any free Saturday evening, we birds of a feather would flock together and shop talk in an eclectic gathering. Actors and actresses, singers and musicians gabbed, sang or played for one another and those not in the arts. Several of the fraternity houses had pianos, and other instruments magically appeared. Everything was played from Bach to Boogie while the atmosphere throbbed with excitement.

Like our studies, our spare time pleasures were stepped up. Friendships formed in a hurry were enjoyed with deeper meaning. We learned to respect the lifetime lived in a few weeks with the knowledge that the scene could change in a wink with an order written on a piece of paper.

A portion of the personnel that participated here were stationed Stateside like myself, with others brought in from overseas and the fighting fronts. We had no idea whether we would be doing our thing here or "over there" since we were subject to relocation. We were given this concentrated training to be able to stage entertainment with any materials at hand—or utilize anything else we could find or requisition.

Lieutenant Edward Stevenson, experienced in motion pictures, was the genius who guided us in the art of creative costuming, wig making and the art of making something out of nothing. Major O'Daniels coaxed non-performers into acting and inspired performers to greater heights with his instruction on the subject of Soldier Shows and exercises in psychodrama.

Even though I had designed fashion ever since I could hold a needle, and had sung, danced, and acted my way through my early years, I gained by this present education and experience at Washington and Lee. We traded secrets and know-how, had no time to waste, and put all that we knew and all that we had learned into practice as soon as possible.

ꙮ

We were taught the "Army way" in the sixth oldest college in the United States and the one to which General Robert E. Lee had been appointed president after the Civil War. The special surroundings in which our classes took place were not lost on me, particularly the lectures held in Lee Chapel on the campus. The same curiosity which put me into uniform thence to strange places and occupations, did not fail to lure me behind the pulpit where stairs led down and around into the dimly lit bowels of the basement museum and its ancient contents.

The atmosphere smelled of history which the musty University Museum was testament to. The Chapel had been constructed under the General's personal supervision as a repository for his personal papers and mementos and was the burial place for him and his immediate family. There, also, reposed articles from the relatives of George Washington, Martha Custis Washington and the Lees. Displayed were ledgers, other items of common use in that day, uniforms and field equipment of soldiers in the Revolutionary War and more.

Few ventured behind the pulpit, but those of us who did were rewarded with reminders of objects that were precious to someone else, of soldiers in wars long past, and what other people, like us, believed in enough to leave hearth and home for.

Lastly, there reposed General Lee. I was touched!

❦

We were granted a weekend holiday break in our intense program of studies because the courses in Personnel Services took place through the Yuletide and New Year. After some hasty debates and quick decisions on the subject of what distances we could cover in the few short days, many of us elected to strike out for our goals near or far—mine was home to Brooklyn, New York.

The Army supplied the conveyances to get us off the college grounds and disperse us to connections for other transportation. Ordered to gather in the early evening at an appointed place, we did. As usual, under these conditions, we waited and entertained one another with jokes and stories to keep our spirits up and stay awake, until sometime in the middle of the night when the buses finally rolled into the depot. We climbed aboard wearily, slumped into our seats and dozed while the vehicles rumbled on their way in the darkness to start us on our elected destinations.

We touched base, if we could, then turned to wend our way back to Lexington. Many such gestures were not easy, but in this case worth it to me when I could throw my arms around the folks at home and have them hug me in return.

❦

In this gathering of people in analogous occupations, interests and age, there were many who were mentally gifted, physically attractive or both. One officer, Lieutenant Abbott, handsomer than most, was appreciated by a number of the female population on the campus. I too was a silent admirer when we came in contact with one another in the course of any day.

One afternoon, this officer asked if he might have private words with me, and we mutually agreed on a time. I was no end curious, while my heart went "pitty-pat." We met in the evening and he "needed an opinion on a personal matter and did I care to give mine?" I did!

The story was this: A friend of his sister's, a girl he had known for many years, and who was now in the Service too, came to the University the day before to visit with him. Later that evening she had revealed that she adored him, and couldn't they be lovers! He was taken aback by her proposal, and what did I think! I then stated my honest opinion to someone whose ego appeared happily well-balanced, and my comments seemed to be absorbed in the same spirit.

Did he care for her at all?

Was there a possibility that he might?

No!—then he would have to state that to her! We agreed that she was truthful and direct in her actions which was an admirable trait. Relieved to have another viewpoint, he thanked me and left, but when he did he took with him that part of myself that was flattered to be consulted and left behind the fragment that made my heart beat faster. "Oh well, there's always tomorrow. . . !"

At a later date, when we had our extravaganza of a show, the Lieutenant was dressed (or shall I say undressed) for the part of an Indian Brave, complete with bronzed body makeup, multi-colored feather headdress that cascaded to the floor, breech-clout and moccasins! He was placed on a platform for all the cast and audience to admire while drums thundered about him and dancers paid him homage—along with the stares of envious males and appreciative females.

❧

Pansy Bates, who was quartered with me, boasted that she made the best biscuits in the South and was homesick for the taste of them. I, not to be outdone suggested butter and marmalade for an accompaniment and scrambled eggs too. We decided bacon and coffee would enhance the biscuits, eggs, butter and marmalade and in agreement, we planned to turn these tasty visions into reality the very next Sunday evening.

The kitchen facilities as well as all cooking equipment in the fraternity houses, were padlocked. We convinced the superintendent who was the keeper of all, that we were really "hausfraus" in uniform, received permission to use the kitchen and were entrusted with the keys. After a review of the contents of our purses, and with grocery list in hand, we made our foray into town.

One cannot make biscuits for two—so we invited a few close friends for this mouthwatering treat, they too had a few friends—hence our resources were stretched as far as they would go. The words "biscuits and scrambled eggs" smacked of home, and snowballed, with the result that the following Sunday, by request, we were in business handling a crowd that materialized from several other areas and who had saved their appetites, it seemed, from the day they entered the Service!

For a short spell we reverted to our traditional roles as housekeepers with a brood to feed. Somehow we begged and borrowed enough wherewithal to sponsor several more soirees for our personal Army, where we ate and chatted happily, then sat about our late night fireplaces and talked, sang or made music.

It was during one of these evening gatherings that I formed a friendship with a talented WAC, a concert singer and educator who was stationed at the Second Service Command Convalescent Hospital in New York. Berenica Rappoport—"Nikki" to all—said to me: "There's only one place for you to be, that's at the Opry House at Camp Upton, we need you!" The "Opry House"? What in the world — ! She explained what they did, the fact that a vacancy existed, and there was a want for my special kinds of work.

After graduation and my return to New Orleans, a request by the Commanding Officer at the Detachment at Camp Upton was routed via Washington DC to Headquarters at Lake Ponchartrain, which resulted in my transfer to fill out the complement at the theater. The 26th of January, 1945, I was packed, and with orders and ration coupons in hand, I headed northward. . . !

The Virginia Rail

This journey to New York was going to be on a circuit grown familiar—one by way of Richmond, Virginia.

Ah! Richmond, I knew it well coming and going across the country. I had great affection for the city. For many of us in uniform, traversing the country, east, west, north and south, our vehicles came chugging through that railroad center which was a hub of activity.

The great switching station was here, where cars were either disconnected from or added to a particular train, and passengers could change to other lines. For me, it was a point at which I was nearing home, or if departing from there, the place where I took a deep breath and settled back for the long ride ahead. If it was in the dark of night, I was tossed and rolled about in my sleeping berth when the coaches were detached and reattached. The sounds of screeching brakes and grinding wheels were comforting since they meant someone was doing his job in the wee hours of the night to get me to my destination.

There were occasions when my connections were delayed, so I passed the idle hours at the USO where I felt at home—notably during the trip from New Orleans to Long Island. I spent a happy time on the premises singing, while a gracious civilian volunteer accompanied me on the piano. On that particular journey I stayed overnight at a hotel in order to get the proper transportation to my new military post.

Yes—I remember Richmond warmly, especially on my last trek from the south to the northeast as a soldier!

April, 1944—At home, left to right, brother Leonard, Clarice, Mother and sister Erma.

July, 1944 at recruiting-bond booth, Clarice and Amelia Sentilles.

Clarice in a photo taken at "Maison Blanche" Department Store, New Orleans, 1944.

Certificate of Graduation

WAR DEPARTMENT   ARMY SERVICE FORCES

SCHOOL FOR PERSONNEL SERVICES

*

This is to Certify that

Corporal CLARICE M. FORTGANG

has satisfactorily completed the prescribed course for

Athletic and Recreation Enlisted Assistants

FOR THE COMMANDANT:

GIVEN AT LEXINGTON, VIRGINIA

THIS 17TH DAY OF JANUARY

A. D. 1945

FREDERICK I. GODSHALK
Lt. Colonel, AUS
ASSISTANT COMMANDANT

Clarice and Dad, New Orleans, summer, 1944.

At the "Opry House" window, 1945, Clarice with (left) "Andy" Anderson and Jay Lundy.

Orchestra and cast members, "Opry House", Camp Upton.

In performance at the "Opry House", Camp Upton, 1945.

VOL 5 NO 13   **FEBRUARY 23, 1945**

USAFI STUDY COURSES OFFER OPPORTUNITIES

Opportunities offered by the United States Armed Forces Institute (USAFI) are knocking at every door in Camp Upton--and receiving a warm welcome.

Among soldiers of the detachment of patients who have enrolled in USAFI courses in recent days are S/Sgt. Jay R. Ackerman, Pvt. Israel Alexander, T/Sgt. Peter C. Belott, Cpl Harris Bloom, Pvt. Joseph A. Burnett, T/5 Joseph Colane, Pvt. Charles R. Dognon, Pvt. John D. DeLuca, T/3 Ernest C. Fascoldt, Pfc George E. Grabowski, Pvt. Harold Greenholtz, Pvt. Richard L. Husted, and S/Sgt. Stanley T. Jackubowski.

Others include Pvt. John J. Keegan, Pvt. Alton Kohlman, Pvt. John H. Leiser, Pvt. Joseph Levine, Pvt. Raymond S. Lowther, Pvt. Harry S. Rozycki, Pvt Leo T. Sarwin, Pfc Anthony F. Tasohler, Sgt. Alexander J. Valentine, and S/Sgt. William Volpe.

Subjects cover almost every field of learning. Those chosen so far by Camp Upton thinkers include American History, Writings
(Continued on Page 4)

ALL CADRE TO WEAR INSIGNIA OF MEDICS

All permanent party personnel assigned to the ASF Convalescent Hospital and the 1234 SCU will wear the lapel insignia of the Medical Corps--the Caduceus--in the future. The insignia will be distributed as soon as it is available.

Permanent party personnel are also reminded that the only shoulder patches to be worn are those of the Second Service Command, the so-called "Ice-Cubes".

LT ELEDGE IS WED TO CAPTAIN HOWELL

St. Valentine's Day again brought echoes of wedding bells to Camp Upton from the marriage of officers stationed here. Lt. Margaret E. Eledge, WAC and Captain Ralph D. Howell, C. E. were the happy couple

Lt. Eledge is a native of Englewood, Tennessee, and a graduate of Carson-Newman college. She has been at Upton since November 1943, and is serving the Post as Signal Officer, Postal Officer and Executive Officer of the WAC Detachment.

Captain Howell's home is at Babylon, LI, where the couple will live. He is a graduate of Pratt Institute Ho is Assistant Post Engineer and NCO Club Custodian

MEATLESS DAYS SET!

Two meatless days a week, in the manner similar to that ordained in the restaurents of the larger cities of the country, will be instituted immediately in Camp Upton's Post Exchanges, Service Club Officers Club and Non Commissioned Officers Club. The action resulted from a directive from Second Service Command Headquarters concerning the critical shortage of meat.

In addition, there is every prospect that the snack munchers at the Officers Club and the Non Commissioned Officers Club will be limited to a steady diet of fish and chips, or cheese, eggs and chicken. A second directive received yesterday bans the sale of meats to these Clubs by the Post Commissary, their sole source of supply.

In line with the first directive, Captain Henry D. Morgan, Post Exchange Officer, has ruled that Saturdays and Sundays will be meatless sandwich days at the Dugout, the Better 'Ole and the Service Club. The plan will go into effect tomorrow.

The Officers Club had planned to be meatless on Wednesdays and Saturdays, and the NCO Club on Saturdays and Sundays until yesterday's order came through.

The Upton Nooz—one of many newspapers published for amusement or information or both, by and for members of the Armed Forces.

WAC detachment from Camp Upton marching at Patchogue, New York, 4 July 1945.

Tuesday, October 23, 1945

Thing of the Past

Army Signal Corps Photo—Cpl Morgenstern

THE OPRY HOUSE

Famed Opry House Folds as Crew Disbands

The long and varied saga of the Opry House, most celebrated show-place in the Army, came to a quiet and undramatic end here recently when the Opry House Players, responsible for many an evening's entertainment, disbanded and were absorbed into other units, leaving the battered birthplace of scores of GI shows to collect dust and memories.

Mecca of thousands of GI theatre-goers during Upton's reception center era and, to a lesser degree, during the early stages of the Convalescent Hospital, the Opry House began its slow disintegration some months ago when, condemned as a fire trap, its stage lights were dimmed forever, and it came into use solely as a rehearsal spot for Opry shows staged elsewhere on the post.

Last Show

It was last used during rehearsals of "Here's How," last production of the Players, which was staged in Theatre 2 early last month and attended by, among others, Major Melvyn Douglas, of screen fame.

Since then, T/4 Gene Marvey, director; Pfc Ed Heisler, tenor; Pfc James Murphy actor-narrator, and P⸍

In costume as "Ado Annie" from "Oklahoma"—with friend, Camp Upton, 1945

COMING FULL CIRCLE

When I arrived at the Camp, I became a member of the 1234th SCU WAC Detachment, the address being shortened from Second Service Command Convalescent Hospital, Camp Upton, New York.

What was now a hospital installation, was originally utilized in both World Wars as a reception and processing center for recruits, from which the men were distributed for Basic Training. Known in World War I as "Camp Upton at Fort Yaphank," the Post became a place for convalescence in the latter part of World War II due to the need for facilities that catered to the care of those returned from overseas.

The present Medical Department was devoted to the diagnosis and treatment of soldiers with psychiatric problems and attended to their bodily wounds as well—one or both being the result of active service. From there the recovered personnel were returned to duty, or discharged.

In connection with this total picture, the Opry House had a special function.

Entertainment yes—but more than that, a place where the recuperating Military might be encouraged to participate with our company musically, theatrically or technically. Although we of the staff were concerned with the mechanics of getting a show on the boards, we were very much involved in the welfare of the patients, some of whom were also professional stage people who came to work with us during their rehabilitation. Others, whose hobby was the theater, or who first wandered into the playhouse to spend an idle hour observing a rehearsal, often stayed to take part in our productions. The mission of our crew was to reinforce a sense that each one had much to give the public. It was heartwarming to perform side by side with someone who had come to our workplace with a loss of assurance or the ability to communicate verbally—then having gained familiarity and confidence in us, insinuated himself into an active role in a show or behind the scene. How many times we members of the troupe watched from the wings with tears in our eyes as a mending GI overcame, or as we stood beside a no-longer shy or frightened partner while all took our bows together—they, sometimes propped by crutches or a cane! These were our moments of satisfaction. This was what we labored to achieve at our branch of the Service.

When I joined the Opry House, there were three other WACs attached there; Nikki Rappoport, who also conducted classes for the Information and Education Department was our resident soprano, Ruth McLarry was a specialty dancer and skit actress and Ruth MacDougal played the trumpet in the orchestra. I became costume designer, all around player and comedienne, and at a later date, Judy Braun, a former vaudevillian rounded out the permanent group.

The men of the company were our director, singer Gene Marvey; assistant to Gene, Ed Kogan; set designer, Bob Aldrich. Additional personnel were actors Sam Main, Jay Lundy and Ed Murphy; Stan Kramien, magician; singer, Ed Heisler; and as music conductor, Philip Fradkin. There were eight staff musicians and on occasion, guest members with their specialty instruments, who swelled the size of the orchestra when needed. The same was true of the cast, which was added to when required. In this assemblage no one was a "star"—we all shared equally in tasks and billing with the complete operation under the auspices of the Special Service Department.

❦

The Opry House site itself dated to World War I, where Irving Berlin, then a celebrated composer and recruit at Upton, wrote, organized and played in the *Yip, Yip, Yaphank* show to raise money for a Post Service Center. Again in 1942, the War Department called on Mr. Berlin, to aid in gathering funds for Army Relief, and as a civilian volunteer he wrote and directed a second musical entitled *This is the Army*, with an all male cast and crew before the Women's Army Corps was a functioning reality.

This show moved from the Opry House to Broadway, followed by tours through the United States and Europe. At long last, several of the original players returned to Upton and composed part of our company.

❦

Our theater troupe functioned on air in an atmosphere where capital was hard to come by, so that materials for our stage dress, wigs and accessories were cagily garnered from various sources. The Quartermaster Department gave me damaged bed sheets and from the Mess Halls came flour bags, both of which I fashioned into costumes or used for props. On Saturdays I canvassed the wholesale millinery, garment and theater districts in Manhattan from whom I collected donations of baubles, bangles, beads and feathers.

On a visit to Radio City Music Hall, I was received by the stage director, Russell Markert, who gave me a generous gift of well-worn satins, laces and spangle-covered items that were reworked into finery for our shows. I prided myself on the fact that I could turn any sow's ear into a silk purse, professionally speaking, and as an example, pantaloons from that source became ruffled Spanish skirts for the show *Hubba Hubba from Trinidad* with under facings that I decorated with sparkling Spanish roses that flashed under the lights. Another time from our own Quartermaster, we received colorful irridescent oilcloth typewriter wrappings in hues that were every jewel shade in the artists' palette; shimmering reds, purples, greens, blues, silvers and golds which provided the inspiration for the glittering Grecian warrior helmets in the musical *P.F.C. Mary Brown*.

Once, the Special Service Office allowed us an appropriation of $75!—a windfall which we of the flour-bag-and-torn-sheet-brigade had never seen before. This princely sum sponsored purchases of supplies for several shows that included a quantity of needed grease paint. Now that we had an adequate store of cosmetics, one member of the troupe suggested makeup cases for each of us, a luxury heretofore not indulged in, whereon we went to the Camp Upton garbage dump and foraged for discarded ammunition boxes which served the purpose very well. We all agreed that having one's own theatrical makeup box bolstered one's self-esteem to civilian professional levels.

Performances took place every two or three weeks depending on required rehearsal time. Appearances took place at the Opry House or at one of the larger post theaters according to the type of show and the estimated audience. In the case of those hospitalized, and others unable to attend—cast, crew and scenery were carried across camp to the Medical Area.

One winter night at the hospital, as we worked on a makeshift stage the front of which was by day the interior side of a loading platform, we ladies, dressed in evening gowns, and the men slightly better off in regulation shirts, exited between scenes to our "backstage," which was in the open air, and where we all stamped our feet and clapped our hands to keep warm. The female contingent, with our arms, chests and backs exposed to the chill, were grateful to have the men blow their hot breath on our spinal columns which enabled us to reappear on the stage with a private shiver—and a public smile!

❦

What entertained our following of Armed Forces men and women?

Burlesque skits, music and dance were the program before my arrival and we continued this successful formula. After my assignment, we were in a position to do the comedy *Three Men on a Horse*, and shows such as *P.F.C. Mary Brown*, (written by three Army men), *Hubba, Hubba from Trinidad* and *Here's How*, which were musicals with a story line. *Here's How*, incidentally, was our last presentation while we were still a company at the old Opry House.

The demands for our services were not all connected with our playhouse work. We performed microphone readings selected by the Information and Education Department that related to its class programs, and for this purpose we did a dramatization of the play *Bury the Dead* by Irwin Shaw, and other contemporary writings.

Our WAC Commandant, Lieutenant Welch, who was very fond of her hardworking "theater WACs," visited us from time to time and added a letter of commendation to my record.

'A Night At the Uproar'
—The G.I. Audience

When my own company was not in a state of preparation, I sometimes attended the motion picture theater, which placed me on the other side of the footlights where, like the local movie house in Nacogdoches, Texas, the audible audience was a feature of each picture or stage show on the Post. These soldiers, away from home and loved ones for great lengths of time, had been wounded physically, psychologically or both, which made them less inhibited than those who had not laid their lives on the line. During any filming, they expressed themselves frankly and volubly to the surrounding listeners. Advice to the actors and directors was given freely and if not entirely agreeable to a fellow viewer, the matter was settled loudly then and there!

These sonorous comments extended to our own theater performances during which opinions expressed were taken by us with good grace and the awareness from whence they came, and since praises aimed in our direction outweighed any adverse criticisms, our efforts were received with the assurance that the Opry troupe could do no wrong. This form of attendance participation was a great outlet for a crowd for whom "letting it all hang out" was a step on the way to recovery.

Our old building eventually showed its age. It had served nobly in World War I and was still in service with us when it became a haven for rodents, and thus was closed for a period to be treated by the Extermination Squad. After that time we were permitted to hold rehearsals, prepare props and scenery and do costume work on the premises, but our appearances took place elsewhere at the Camp.

ॐ

We who were attached to the entertainment section were close friends and spent many off hours together at the Service Club during the week and away from our station on weekends. Ed Kogan and his wife, Martha, had a studio suite in Greenwich Village where we gathered some Saturday evenings. We brought snacks and sodas, relaxed and laughed about the week that was, and chewed bubble gum—the biggest bubble won the day! On summer evenings, all of us sauntered from the Kogans' to the East River where we sat along the pier and dangled our feet in the water. At other times we met at the Sammy Mains' apartment also in the Village area, in a suite of rooms formerly occupied by John Barrymore, which was a place of conviviality and a refuge from the "uniform" week at Upton.

Nikki Rappoport and her husband, Israel, were my hosts too in their apartment near Columbia University. The location of their address made for colorful food purchases with a choice of Italian, Puerto Rican and other gastronomic delights which we enjoyed together because we shared a gusto for ethnic foods.

Weekends our hearts were on loan to the civilian population but by the dawn of Monday, when the dulcet tones of Reveille sounded, we could be found back on the Post in our separate barracks, all lined up on our cots under olive drab blankets labeled—"U.S. Army."

A WAC AT CAMP UPTON

Always soldiers, we were roused from our sleep by the bugle aided by the First Sergeant's lively urgings, whereon we fell out and started the day in the prescribed soldierly style. When we departed for work, our quarters were always left ready for inspection.

The WACs here were assigned to a variety of jobs not offered in earlier enlistments. While the War progressed and needs became many, so the scope of vocations broadened. At this medical post, friends performed tasks in the psychiatric, nursing, surgi-technical and medical-clerking departments. Some were situated in the Dental, Opthalmic and allied healing fields, also in Physical and Occupational Therapy. Other women went about their duties at locations in the various Camp offices where they conducted the activities necessary to keep any installation running and its morale high.

❦

We could choose to walk or ride on the mini buses to our place of employment. For our group occupied at the Opry House, we often walked or rode there together. There were long days with no nine-to-five jobs in mind and when readying a show, we hustled to the theater earlier in the morning than other occupations required, then back to the barracks for lunch, followed by mail call. We returned to work in the afternoon and finished at all hours. If we arrived late for the last meal of the day, whatever was available was served to us by the cooks and Mess staff. The food was plain, wholesome and plenteous.

The atmosphere at the Detachment offered little incentive to spend time there after work other than necessary shoe polishing, laundering, letter writing, etc. Outside of those obligations we shopped at the PX, attended a motion picture or USO show or socialized in congenial company at the Service Club which had the homey air of a Company Parlor. For the male soldiers we met there in the evening we women again represented mother, sister, sweetheart and friend and all could enjoy conversation and dancing in this fair exchange of companionship.

Additional leisure hour choices were bowling or basketball games where WAC units competed with women's teams from other Military bases, USO athletic groups, local business sports associations and our own men's leagues. Trips to Fire Island for horseback riding, were available to us, and in the hot weather, there was transportation to the beaches for swimming. Since we were near enough to New York City to get there conveniently, personnel and patients who were permitted to leave, took advantage of this option on weekends.

ॐ

There were several ways to get off the Post. The most desirable was to own a car or prearrange for a ride. Another was to walk toward the exit gate with the proper pass in hand and hope a driver headed away from Camp would stop and offer a ride. The last was the use of the thumb, which on military grounds was a "no-no," but was an accepted method once outside the immediate area.

Trips with fellow soldiers were the kinds I had most often,

but sometimes the ones that were not, were lessons in a philosophical view of life. For instance, at the start of one weekend, a friend and I walked on the road where we hoped to hitch a ride, whereon we were invited into a chauffeured limousine with a lone woman the occupant of the back seat. We uttered a few polite words of thanks, which were received curtly—from there on the lady ignored us totally and conversed only with her chauffeur while we sat staring and silent, suppressing the desire to laugh at the humor of the situation. At other times, when rides were offered, congeniality was the order of the day and a warm feeling in such an exchange was a good start for the end of the week.

If we planned to use the train on any of these journeys, the trip was by military bus and the Island transit routes. The Jamaica Station in Long Island City was the junction for travel connections and with few exceptions we changed there, sometimes at our inconvenience. On arrival at that location, we could exit from our cars and dash into the departing ones with barely seconds to spare, or inversely, we waited hours for the proper links. On our return, with the precious passes stretched as far as they could go, we traveled via the same Long Island Railroad line late at night and only half awake.

These episodes led to a like situation incorporated into one of our shows; that was, the probability that any Sunday evening in a somnolent state we might wander into the wrong car at the station in Jamaica and land in some strange place—Trinidad?—it was possible! From this idea *Hubba Hubba from Trinidad* was born with these play lines between two GIs on the island: "How did you get here?" the reply, "I took the wrong train in Jamaica," and with a sigh, the pensive agreement, "So did I!" — which brought an enormous response from the uniform-clad house!

And So to Sleep —?

There came an end to every day, and some bedtime preparations lent variety to the scene. My early observation that we were from every walk of life and there was much to learn about one another had an additional aspect. While we women routinely undressed for retirement and donned our pajamas, two WACs, who were the exception, were usually observed in the process of "dressing up" for their sleep. These ladies outfitted themselves in undergarments beneath their pajamas, and in addition added skirts, jackets and raincoats over those. "What," we asked ourselves, "could they be doing!"

The story related by their close neighbors was this: these girls, whose roots were in rural areas, had their first opportunity to own the quantity and quality of clothing distributed by the Women's Army Corps. The desire to hold on tightly to this wealth prompted a round-the-clock method of security by which the two wore extra sets of underwear, shirts and skirts during the work day and at nighttime.

The discovery of what took place each evening brought to mind that early time in Seattle when my group, freshly arrived via Oglethorpe, Georgia, and Nacogdoches, Texas, exchanged stories with our compatriots from Fort Devens, Massachusetts who had settled in shortly before us. They too, had dressed for their nocturnal rest during Basic Training in New England, where the temperatures fell so low during the cold of winter, that each woman donned quantities of her under and outer garments to survive the chill in the unheated barracks! For reasons so diverse did our mountain girls and they, bed down in everything they owned.

ೞ

No tales of the night can be complete without the prayerful appeal that begins—"Now I lay me down to—!"

Girls will be girls and man must have his mate, to which we add another truism "there are a few in every barrel." In the enormity of the warfare effort, they were as fly specks in the ointment; we had two of these "flies" in our Company. Each time the venereal disease count surged upward in the male area of the Camp, a call was heard over the loudspeaker for these particular "ladies of the evening" to report to the office. We had all the triumphs of a gigantic number of people with their shoulders to the wheel for this gargantuan campaign to win the War—and its human failings too!

❦

The classical Dantean phrase . . . "who from a dream awakened" recalls an incident in and about our WAC unit housing.

After a weekend off, one of the girls returned from home with her dog named Mary, an Australian breed, that had the bashful, dainty, skittish qualities of a maiden aunt. What the rules and regulations might be regarding her presence on the grounds, was never ascertained by us. Mary, who remained contentedly beneath her owner's cot, would peep out and about and occasionally venture forth, but if anyone came her way during her mild excursions, she shyly turned away and retreated to her place under the bed.

Had she been more aggressive, there were times we could have used a stout bark and bite to repel some uninvited visitors—members of the vast numbers of male personnel. These men who had returned lately from the fighting fronts and their attempted sorties in the direction of the WAC barracks, created a condition which necessitated patrols around our quarters.

The would-be invaders were resourceful. One climbed to

the second story in the dark of night and caused a commotion in his attempt to molest a girl there, and instead
alerted the whole floor instantly. On another occasion a
soldier used the direct approach—the front door, from
whence he strolled through the center aisle of our beds
and was spotted by the light sleepers, the foremost being
myself, with the result that my high "F" led all the rest
of the screaming which shortly put the intruder in the
hands of our Military Patrol.

All this commotion with not even a bark from Mary!
Well!—I for one, wouldn't count on *her* again!

— And in the Morning

Our closeness and concern for each others' feelings were
ever present due to the circumstance of the conflict and
the openness in our lifestyle. It didn't take much to remind
us of our nearest and dearest from whom we were separated
and for whose safe return we prayed silently, or openly,
and whom we discussed every day in the week, and every
week in the year.

One dawn that followed a severe winter night in our
chilly barracks on Long Island, we commented on the cold
and talked to one another about how we had huddled into
our blankets. One had added an extra covering, and another had piled on two, and her coat atop of those—then
a pause, and from a far corner came a wistful, "Yes, but
one husband is warmer than seven blankets!"— to which
thought there were agreements voiced by the married ladies in our quarters. . . !

These moments spurred us on, kept ever fresh in our
minds the reasons why we worked in 24-hour-day shifts
and why we weren't going to slacken that pace until those
husbands, brothers, fathers, friends, and sweethearts were
with us again!

❦

In the Service, there were situations that came about
in the name of comradeship that could involve one in circumstances other than the workplace. One of these
parodied the old axiom, "a little learning is a dangerous
thing . . ." here related with a twist to it; i.e., "a little
conceit is a necessary attribute—too much conceit can be
a total bust!"

Nikki, with whom I had an intimate friendship, and great
admiration for as singer and teacher, possessed a vanity
that matched her skills which led to a predicament more
uncomfortable for her than for me. A background to this
event was the fact that we bore little physical resemblance
to one another. Even though I was taller, with facial features very different and unlike eyes and coloring, we were
ofttimes mistaken by the soldier public, and after our shows
were congratulated on each other's performances.

There were many talented military men at Camp Upton,
amongst them a photographer whom Nikki came to know,
and as his work became familiar to her and she gained confidence in his abilities, she arranged to have a portrait done.
During the sitting at the off-post studio, Nikki became en-
raptured with his artistry and efforts, then with her upper
torso covered in a shawl, grew so enthusiastic, that as the
fabric was draped this way and that to her liking, it was,
in the course of time, dropped from one breast and then the
other for a more elegant phase of the camera session.

She afterward was ecstatic about how well the procedure
had gone and looked forward to seeing the proofs. What
Nikki was not aware of was the first viewing of them was
not exclusively for the subject's eyes alone, but that the
photographer considered it a lark to show the proofs to
his colleagues and friends at Camp Upton even before she
could see them.

Half nude she had made a big hit with the male population! Eventually, she viewed the photos and I did too. We agreed that they were skillfully done but too risqué for the atmosphere of the Post, and would lead to unwelcome gossip. To head off the ensuing havoc, I suggested that since people generally mistook the two of us anyway, we might exaggerate their bewilderment and take the sting out of the cameraman's game if we styled our hair the same, wore the exact outer garments and walked to and from all activities together, for an allotted time.

Nikki concurred, and that is what we did. The would-be "to-do" soon died down.

❦

Life was not all khaki, and if there was a uniform sameness about us, I for one looked for the "different." Beneath our apparent olive drabness there lived a life of flaming color which came about when I brought to the barracks items that needed to be dyed for a show. On a whim, I added with them, a few pieces of my own lingerie. The outcome was a giant-hued success! Requests for sundry undies to be tinted for my friends resulted in an effect that happily varied the fawn browns and olive drabs. Thereafter we went about our business as usual with blooming violet girdles and glowing ruby red or emerald green bras under our issues of khaki slips.

There was still another occasion to diversify the tone of the tan and putty existence for the WACs at Detachment Headquarters which occurred during the time when I designed the many gowns for the *PF.C. Mary Brown* show. I did not join the cast in this musical, but worked behind the scenes to complete the numbers of costumes required. It provided the opportunity for some of my friends in my detachment to wear evening dresses and I felt a special pleasure in furnishing the means for our ladies to appear their most feminine in a fashion show that lent a dazzling splash of color!

My furlough at that period of 1945 afforded an entertaining way to vary my own routine military apparel and accompanying responses. My usual day spent learning lines, songs, and doing costumes, had a radical change of pace and place on that vacation which I spent at a dude ranch in upstate New York in Western garb. How anyone chose to spend an authorized holiday was a personal matter. Two of our women announced that they had requested their leaves at "coon huntin' time" and described the delights of this sport before departing, and more enthusiastically on their return—while others told of heartwarming reunions on distant Indian reservations.

In February of 1945, the *Upton Nooz* and the *Daily Bulletin*, two of the newspapers on the Post, were additional reminders that life was not all "Yes Sir," "No M'am" and olive drab. Motion picture reviews and announcements of coming attractions for the month included: *Having a Wonderful Crime* featuring Pat O'Brien, Carole Landis and George Murphy, *Thunderhead—Son of Flicka*, *Hanover Square* with Laird Cregar and George Sanders, and *Molly and Me* with players Gracie Fields and Monty Woolley.

Listed too were bowling, tennis, baseball and basketball games, arts and crafts exhibits, the appearance of Shakespearian actress and director, Margaret Webster, who was scheduled to speak, and notice was served that two meatless days a week were now in effect at our Post Exchanges, Service Clubs and snack places to cooperate with emergency shortages.

We read that the insignia we wore on our upper left sleeve was to be changed from the double white cubes on blue, denoting the Second Service Command, to the Caduceus, the sign of the Medical Corps. These were to be distributed to all personnel upon receipt of the items. (The shipment never materialized and our shoulder patches remained the white on blue cubes!)

The Information and Education Section held discussions

on current events, and courses were offered for those who could attend, which included studies in American History, Writings of American Authors, Business English, Aviation Engines, Bookkeeping and Accounting, Metallurgy, Blueprint Reading and many more. Gossip columns recorded the progress of romances within the offices of the various departments and the comings and goings of people, both civilian and military. Our show, *Band Frolics* when reviewed, was said to have "made a hit with the Opry House crowds" who attended the performances.

The success of our playhouse and its innovative place in rehabilitation was taken note of by our Service Command, whereon that agency dispatched interested officers to observe our mode of operation. A member of that group was Major Melvyn Douglas, known to the motion picture public, who, during one dress rehearsal questioned me as to where I had garnered our generous quantity of costume supplies. The Major and his party then took a closer look and were surprised to see that flour bags, damaged sheets, donations from Radio City Music Hall and the New York garment district were what I had to work with. From a respectable distance the wardrobe appeared to have cost a goodly sum!

At a later date, a combination civilian-service team composed of four people a writer, actor, and two composers, was sent by the Service Command to create a show for us and spent many weeks at our theater. Their efforts resulted in the musical, *Here's How*, which we afterward performed. The four were Alex North and Elie Siegmeister, composers, Alice Marks, writer, and Art Smith, stage and screen actor—and thereby hangs a tale of adventure.

During one of the forementioned weekend return trips to Camp via the Long Island Railroad, Art Smith and I were amongst the many on the train as it chugged along the regular late-night route into the town of Patchogue. We then all boarded the bus which became disabled on its way to Upton. After due consideration, it was announced that we could not proceed, were in the middle of nowhere in the pitch dark, and that someone would have to go on foot for aid which would take hours.

Art Smith, whom I knew only slightly, told me he would lead me to where we could get assistance and make our way back to the Post, or at least get some lodging. In the invisibility of the moonless expanse, with Art preceding and holding tightly to my hand, we stumbled through fields, crossed over roads, pushed through brambles, walked north, east, south and west. During all this time there was not a glimmer of light or a building in sight as I followed in blind faith through the blackness of the opaque veil.

Art persisted and said he knew where we were going although it seemed as if we had walked to the end of Long Island. Suddenly a beam appeared ahead of us in the murk, and we approached a huge Victorian house of a sort used for summer retreats in days long gone, which elicited an "Aha!" from my companion. He then told me what he was certain he would find—it was the home of Elie Siegmeister, a member of the composing team—and we had come to the end of our wanderings.

The Siegmeisters welcomed us warmly, we could then relax and laugh about the tenseness we had endured feeling our way to their home. A sidelight of our adventure was the discovery that Mrs. Siegmeister and I were distantly related since a branch of her family were Fortgangs too!

In that huge residence with its rabbit-warren of rooms, they found places to house us comfortably, and I, subject to Army rules, made contact with my detachment by telephone and explained the situation lest I be considered AWOL (an infraction punishable by Court Martial); after which we all retired for the evening.

With the dawn of morning when our surroundings were divested of their mysterious nighttime's shroud, Art Smith, Elie Siegmeister and I prepared to drive back to Camp.

Outdoors in the light of day, the immediate environment appeared to be the setting for a turn-of-the-century drama set in sand and crabgrass, with the house a many-gabled haunting monument to the period.

❦

If the preceding was an unusual experience, the following was a startling episode.

One time, in the afterglow of a performance, Nikki and I started back to our quarters on foot. Since there was a good distance to cover, we proceeded in the hush of the darkness and chatted softly to one another while we relaxed in the confidence and security we felt everywhere on the Post, when shortly we became aware of rustling sounds in the greenery that lined the walk next to us. We paused wordlessly, our eyes met, we agreed not to verbalize our thoughts, and instead continued to walk and talk casually. When the undertones in the plantings increased, we both approached an unvoiced panic and were rigid with fright—then next to us the crackling of the branches accelerated sharply, and suddenly from behind them stepped an enlisted man!

His immediate presence and wild look turned us cold with apprehension, for it was obvious he was in a disturbed state. He asked hesitantly if he could accompany us and seemed fearful that we would refuse, so as calmly and graciously as possible, we accepted his offer. Nikki and I struggled for composure while the hackles rose on our necks—and the three of us continued toward our destination. After several attempts and with our encouragement, the soldier blurted out the cause of his agitation!

He and his buddies had heard that they and other returning GIs were not fit to associate with the girls they had left at home because their experiences had rendered them unsuitable for civilized society. This was from a news interview with our first lady, Eleanor Roosevelt (a statement out of context). We assured him we were proud and honored to be with him which was the truth, and were the words we felt would help to restore his damaged ego. At our front door, he thanked us for tolerating his company!

"Tolerating his company"—we could have burst into tears to think how much of his life he had sacrificed on our behalf. We who had not been called upon to give "the last full measure" or whose state of mind had not been stretched to the breaking point!

We wanted him to know we could never thank him enough!

༡

There were regular news releases from the theaters of combat with sometimes unfounded rumors of bold victories on various fronts until the middle of May 1943, when the Allied armies in North Africa pounded the enemy into submission. Thereafter we concentrated our efforts against the Italians and Germans on their European sites, whereon our invasion of Italy brought about the capitulation of most of that territory in the same year— with the exception of a small portion in the north. Their Fascist dictator, Benito Mussolini, was then imprisoned by his countrymen but was rescued by his German allies who set him up as head of a puppet regime in the upper region. When the Nazi German forces there collapsed in the spring of 1945, he fled, was captured and put to death at the end of April!

In the same month, the city of Berlin fell to our Russian allies which terminated the existence of the German Third Reich and its leader, Adolph Hitler. The Nazi High Command retreated to Denmark where they signed a paper of surrender on the 29th of the month, but word of their defeat did not reach all the Axis armies immediately, so pockets of them fought on until the last of them were overwhelmed and taken prisoner by the 7th of May.

Tuesday morning, the 8th of May, information was broadcast on the radio simultaneously by the governments of the United States, the Soviet Union, England and France, that the Germans had finally given up. This day became "Victory over Europe" or "V-E Day," all details of which were relayed to us immediately via the loudspeaker system on the Post!

Our sights then focused wholly on the theater of the Far East, namely Japan and environs, where the fighting had been ongoing, and which nation was the third party in the Axis. With renewed determination, we took deep breaths, estimated what the job would entail and pushed on!

❦

As summer approached, we prepared for the Fourth of July commemoration to take place in the village of Patchoque, Long Island. Our Commanding Officer planned to head our detachment when we marched, and in the absence of a second in command, she requested that I walk behind her, and the rest of the unit follow us. The Armed Forces portion of the parade was kept to a modest number especially by our Second Service Command Convalescent Hospital which was not in a position to supply numerous troops.

We WACs had been on review in basic training, military schools, army bases and in cities, but treading the pavement in a small town had an air of intimacy that urban areas lacked. On that July day, we marched through the center of Patchoque accompanied by Scout troops, school bands and patriotic organizations. Stray dogs wandered in and out about us and children skipped along beside us. The public on the sidelines demonstrated enthusiastically that we belonged to them—it was a proud moment for the

Women's Army Corps and Upton. When finished, we broke ranks, piled into trucks and took our tired feet back to the barracks.

Were we going to walk in parades forever? When would this all be over? Today? Tomorrow? Next week? In a year?

THE BEGINNING OF THE END

The month of August began with the celebration of my birthday. My brother, still in service, had a bouquet of flowers delivered to me which conveyed the sense of being very special because of the wartime setting and the fact that Camp was many miles from the nearest florist. In the five days that followed, we all went about our regular occupations until the late afternoon of the sixth, when a violent explosion hurtled us into the new age of the atom bomb with word that one had been dropped by our Air Forces on the city of Hiroshima, Japan! Breathlessly we awaited developments. Two days afterward the same kind of deadly discharge was detonated over the town of Nagasaki on the island of Kyushu. Additionally, Russia declared war on Japan and joined the Allies in their efforts to defeat the remaining Axis army.

With both cities totally devastated and the certainty that the enemy was now too crippled to continue, our combined governments offered terms of surrender. On the tenth of the month, members of the Japanese Far Eastern High Command agreed to accept our conditions, but when there was no further word from them by the 13th of August, Allied Air Forces in a concentrated effort, bombed them repeatedly and threatened to loose another atomic missile.

As each communique arrived, the Base became electric with expectation. "Hoping" had become a way of life for so long that the termination of the conflict seemed a dream, a dream ever present without the daring to imagine what

our reactions would be if and when it occurred.
The actuality of the end of the War burst upon Camp Upton on Tuesday, the 14th of August! The news of the capitulation of the Japanese was broadcast immediately over the loudspeaker where the announcer repeated again and again the unreal words! "The War is over!"—"The War is over!" "The Japanese have surrendered!" — !

How can one express the first disbelief, the mounting belief, then the whirling emotions and the intensifying elation! The news flashed like lightning to near and far corners of the installation. Work stopped, the whole station started to have another life, conversations buzzed, voices grew louder. By the approach of evening, celebration had taken over while men and women roamed the grounds, hugged, kissed, sang and shouted. There was little military order! Necessary services continued; for the rest, work was halfhearted.

By sundown, the efforts of the Commanding Officers were focused toward containing the jubilant soldiers by having a place for them to gather with facilities that offered a platform for announcements and room for rejoicing—so during the evening the speaker system directed everyone to the main playhouse on the Post and requested that members of the Opry House company go to the theater. Outside, we walked there in bunches, bands and herds. My acting troupe and our musicians joined one another on the stage! We performed every specialty we could think of—songs, dances, and comic routines that we shouted over the babbling crowd that filled the seating area and wandered in and out. The audience was a blur of movement during which time our superiors urged us to keep going.

This eventful time was immediately tagged V-J Day, short for Victory over Japan Day—and we were up through the night too exhilarated to retire to our barracks.

A memorable occasion—an unforgettable tumult of emotions!

The dream had exploded into being! The reality of it would take somewhat longer to absorb!

Cease and Disband!

In early September, a few short weeks after the momentous victory day, we presented the show *Here's How* and were formulating plans for the work that would follow, when word came through channels for us to stop everything pending judgment on the future of our operation. We found ourselves in a state of uncertainty. Consideration was being given as to how necessary was the function of our unit in the changing picture of Camp Upton. The personnel returned from overseas for treatment were being discharged—our audience was dwindling.

In preparation for our next effort, I had completed wigs, accessories and portions of wardrobe. These pieces hung in rows beneath stickers marked with the names of the actors who would wear them. All of us reported as usual each day, gazed at them and one another, and studied our scripts while we speculated.

We had not long to wait; within the week orders came through moving each of us to various other departments. I was assigned to the Patients' Personnel Office.

The building was abandoned!

❦

I left the Opry House with the rows of wigs and partially made costumes hanging where they were. They represented a circumstance in history never to be repeated, something that had created a life of its own, now ended, and I had been a part of it. There was pride and sadness in these thoughts that made giving up the old theater a wrenching experience. For me the echoes would not fade! The lines and laughs, songs and applause, the struggle for the wherewithal to put on the next show and the next — ! I could see fragments of all I had participated in and those that had taken place in the old showhouse before my era.

There was Irving Berlin directing *Yip Yip Yaphank* with his all male company—painted, padded and kicking their hairy legs as chorus girls in June of 1918. The cast of *This is the Army* in 1942, preparing for that show with the little "Sad Sack" soldier in an oversized uniform—again it was Irving Berlin performing his own "Oh How I Hate to Get Up in the Morning," just as he had in 1918.

Lastly, there we were, men and women soldiers singing and dancing in revues, acting in the comedies *Della Stallas*, *Three Men on a Horse* or doing the musical *PF.C. Mary Brown* and more!

Our weekly newspaper, *The Cadence* featured a photograph of the Opry House on the front page with a summary of the work of our troupe. The history of the playhouse was detailed, and included Irving Berlin's association with it in two World Wars, Major Melvyn Douglas' visit with his party, and mentioned the team who had co-authored and composed *Here's How* for us. The conclusion of the story expressed the mournful feelings of many on the occasion of the closing of "the most celebrated showplace in the Army" and went on to say, "like Abraham Lincoln, it belongs to the Ages."

❦

Now I was needed elsewhere and would give my best to my next assignment at another section where troops, returned from the fighting fronts, were processed for discharge.

In my new work in the Patients' Personnel Office, I scanned documents for all battle and campaign commendations, medals and distinctions merited by the men, and gave those items we had on hand to the appropriate recipients—the remainder to be sent to the veterans when they became available.

Some of the men accepted the honors due them as a matter of course, while others understandably refused them or bitterly threw them down on my desk—but I was not there to reason why, just as I had not been called upon to lay down my life! At such moments the task was more difficult and I hoped the tears that welled in my eyes would not spill over at the wrong moment!

THE FINAL SALUTE

Thanksgiving Day of 1945 had added significance since it carried with it the realization that it would be the last one most of us would spend in the Service, thus would become legend. And now that some friends had already been discharged, the rest of us drew closer.

While we set the tables with paper placemats and small turkey candles, I recalled commemorations at my quarters in Seattle, where at Halloween I surrounded our dining area with cornstalks as paper pumpkins and witches flew through the air—and how for Thanksgiving, Pilgrim and Indian children flirted or played tag, as Indian Braves with hatchets chased the dinner turkeys around the walls. I recollected thoughts of New Orleans at this time of year, when a meal was served Army style—and presently at Camp Upton, there was to be another regulation mode of celebration in our Mess Hall—with one great difference—we would give thanks the hostilities and bloodshed were over! There would be fewer of us at the festive board because of the liberal number of passes issued for the triumphant after-war holiday. For this special season, and in honor of the end of the conflict, an illustrated digest of the Convalescent Hospital was issued. The booklet included our holiday menu, listed all soldier personnel on the Post at that period, and reviewed current and past activities. Photos from the various departments showed the Women's Army Corps at work and leisure and featured the Opry House crew in rehearsal and performance. The booklet served as a later history of

Camp Upton showing the part the station played in the recovery of the physically and mentally wounded.

❧

Before the Christmas-New Year season of 1945, the various offices planned parties at restaurants off the Post to celebrate together for the purpose of enjoying one another's company in places other than military. The undercurrent of parting was there while pictures were taken for mementos.

It all reminded me of the recent past, when in the State of Washington I canvassed the area around our Headquarters for paints, glitter, and holly berries. I could see the walls of the Mess Hall alive with the angels I had painted that appeared to be tiptoeing about in the flickering candlelight. I recalled Lexington, Virginia, and how after an early dinner we had dashed off to await the buses that would take us to wherever we might go in the short recess from the Personnel Services course at the New Year time of 1944.

This particular week of the 25th of December, I spent on the Post where I took my turn at Charge of Quarters and assisted in our office. It was my habit to remain on duty during Christmas and Easter, which allowed those of other faiths the time to celebrate their religious days, as I was free to do the Jewish Holy Days.

❧

The atmosphere in which we functioned had changed and I, for one, felt a precariousness in the air since any morning, noon or evening could be the time of notice of termination of our enlistments. Like treading on water, each daybreak dawned uncertainly awaiting that moment, but I gave my work my utmost attention, no matter what my state of service! The bulletin board was scanned regularly because of ritual, and to see if there was a separation roster and whose names were on it. On the 11th of January a notice was posted for a group to be discharged, and I was listed among them. The axe had fallen!

My state of anticipation had found its crest. I lived from there on in moods of glad and sad. Discharge notices were received by everyone with mixed emotions, for the Army was now home and habit for us, with a routine grown familiar and a lifetime crammed into three years.

❦

During the period I prepared to leave I felt that I was undergoing changes. On and off through my mind floated images of another life which looked familiarly unfamiliar! In the course of those late days at Camp Upton, pictures of myself in civilian clothing rippled through my mind. I became conscious of a loss of distinction, that sense of pride I had in my uniform when amidst the non-military population—there had been so few of us in the female part of the Armed Forces compared with the vast numbers of men.

❦

Friends had been mustered out, but not all the women I knew readied to say farewell to the WAC—because we were offered the option of staying, these ladies had chosen the Army as a career. Why then had I not elected to stay? That determination was made according to one's nature, and my spiritual and psychological home was not in the military unless I was needed to serve during the urgency of war.

❦

The 17th of January was the date our collective was to depart for Fort Dix, the nearest discharge point. At dawn, we were transported by truck from Long Island to Trenton, New Jersey, and the Fort Dix separation area which was to be the place of our "last hurrah!"

The process of release was eased for me by the fact that my brother Leonard was now part of the Fort post personnel. The next evening, he, with his buddies, called for me at my temporary quarters and we celebrated with a feast at Lorenzo's Restaurant in Trenton where we ordered steak entrees, a privilege reserved for the Armed Forces by the owner, since meat was rationed—and thereby occurred a memorable incident. The generous portions were a treat which we soldiers could appreciate with our customary gusto. Leonard was forced to give up before all of his food was finished, and with a look of amused agreement between us, he placed his leftover meat on my plate. When I came to the end of mine, I continued eating and dispatched his too because I reasoned that such bounty should not be relegated to an ignoble end!

My brother's astonishment was total—whereon I became a legend in my own time!

❦

The dinner was a pleasant memory by the following morning when the process of discharge was started.

Rules and regulations required that we return all uniform gear to the Quartermaster Depot, with the exception of one complete outfit to wear en route to our civilian destination. We proceeded up the line until two of us remained. I persuaded the sergeant in charge that my summer cottons and additional winter uniform with raincoat, overcoat and accessories, were of better use in my possession than in his, because there would not be many WACs to require them. After several rounds of palavering, he agreed and did the same for a friend who was with me, thereby we left the Service with more articles than usually allowed.

The following day, the ongoing procedure included a physical examination with medical history noted from enrollment in New York City, until this date. Not much had changed, for on exiting the Service, we again walked about draped in sheets and each grasped jars of urine specimens as we had when we entered. Next were questions about length of service, furloughs, schools attended, the stations at which we had been posted and duties at each location.

The soldier who recorded the numbers assigned to my military employment described them as:

#521 WAAC Basic Training

#070 Draughtsman

#274 Publications Writer

#442 Entertainment Specialist

#405 Recruiter

I continued to add to the list when he informed me that he had filled the allotted space and "how about we call it quits," which we did. Omitted from the calendar was Administrative Specialist, Special Services Non-Commissioned Officer, and Public Relations person. The jobs were lumped together under #442 that showed Entertainment Specialist to be my principal Army occupation. Finances were detailed, and included what was owed to me in salary, transit money to my home, and severance pay.

On the last day of the mustering out process, I was given my release papers with extra plasticized copies of the same reduced to wallet size. I tucked them into my purse with a caution from the dispensing sergeant that they be put in a safe place. I received $3.95 in travel pay and $138.15 which took care of wages and separation fee. A "lame duck" pin was issued to wear in my lapel to signify that I had served in the Military—and I was then free to go! I was "out" on the 19th of January, 1946.

A civilian in uniform!

❦

What did my final papers look like and what were they composed of?

The primary page was headed "Army of the United States," under this the Eagle insignia of the United States, then my name, grade, the place where I was discharged, and in addition attested to my "Honest and Faithful Service to this Country."

The reverse side listed my home address, last civilian school attended, type of Armed Forces Service (WAC) and again the station from which I left. Itemized under medals and citations due were three: Good Conduct Medal, World War II Victory Medal, American Service Medal and one citation, the WAAC Service Ribbon. The Military schools I had attended were noted, monetary payments duly made to me, the state of my Army insurance, and days lost under any infractions of the regulations—of which there were none—were all recorded. On a second page, again with the logo of the United States Army and the Eagle crest, was the Separation Qualification Record that served two purposes. First, for the permanent account of duties performed during the War and second, a resume for any civilian position. The back of this page detailed my pre-volunteer business in antiques and a description of the work involved. The final item was a notation of the length of time served in the Women's Army Auxiliary Corps before I entered the Army of the United States and again described my decorations and citations.

Contained in these two documents was a personal history that accounted for three years of my life.

❦

On the way home, floating in a realm between military and civilian, I mused on the fact that I would feel the want of companionship about me morning, afternoon and evening. My mind dwelt on the murmur of many voices, the friendly exchanges, and those from whom I learned invaluable lessons. I thought of the sundry I had marched shoulder to shoulder with, whose comfort I sought and had given the same in return. I already felt the loss of that womankind, who in trying times rose to admirable heights of stature and endurance. I reflected too on our many officers, who unheralded and unsung, cared deeply and performed difficult jobs while they made wartime life tolerable for those that served under them.

Amongst these laudable ladies were exceptions however and one of these individuals could demoralize a detachment with misused authority, thereby creating unease and mistrust.

I would not miss the presence of any of rank that found the Service a platform from which to mold a situation to their advantage, or created a circumstance where competence was replaced with incompetence to benefit their purpose. I also became wary of an officer whose manufactured Court Martial offenses came about by night prowling in search of WACs in violation of the lesser codes, such as sans their caps or with jackets unbuttoned, because some women had to accept the public humiliation that resulted from these minor infractions. The quoted examples were few in number, but their influence was great on the morale of the affected companies.

Remembered too was a recruiting assignment where the effort to swell our corps was sabotaged by the archaisms: "War is man's work" and "Woman's place is in the home." Enemy propaganda, which we battled regularly, was calculated to throw discredit on the WAC and weaken the Allied cause by deliberately misinterpreting our aims, attacking our moral ethics, emphasizing the dictum of "woman's place," and labeling us "camp followers." Some members of our fighting forces were influenced to relay their disapproval against their ladies donning uniforms, as was the civilian population, since they too had been infiltrated—another disruption in our efforts toward enlistment. We struggled to "overcome" while we went about our work and finally became an accepted part of the team that triumphed.

When traditionally only men left their homes to make the world safe for democracy, I was fortunate to be among those who believed that the pursuit of freedom was likewise a female mission. It was a privilege to be present during the transformation of the male outlook that brought the Women's Army Corps side by side with, and marching to, the same beat as those time-honored soldiers.

❦

What changes had taken place in the area of opportunities offered to females in the Military during the period of my association with the WAC in the Second World War?

We early volunteers, restricted to three choices of assignment: the kitchen, office or motor transport, saw in a short span of time, a century of evolution in the employment of our talents. Through demonstrations of our competence, we found entry into every task the Armed Forces had to offer, short of the battlefield. For example: my colleagues who worked on the piers, soon expanded to sending civilians, nurses, other WACs and male soldiers in and out of the country. They subsequently handled all needed inventory that included guns and ammunition for the men, and saw to it that returning soldiery, enlisted and commissioned, were properly equipped and on the right trains to various camps for return to action, medical care or discharge.

Our ladies were occupied in the Postal Battalions where all "V" mail letters were censored and sent to their destinations. Other jobs included work in water, rail, motor vehicle and mechanical maintenance, salvage, photo labs, mess and supply depots. They scrutinized tons of manifests, cargo reports and convoy lists and were Multigraph operators, supply technicians, tailors and movie projectionists. The ones stationed aboard hospital ships acted as guides, medical admitting staff and finance assistants for the wounded and some were radio operators, medical technicians and nurses aides. WACs who attended the School for Personnel Services as I did, conducted discussions about veterans benefits, discharge procedures and wrote and distributed news sheets; in addition, they were responsible for morale and so supplied music and variety shows. Overseas, women of the Transportation Corps routed war supplies, while others of the Ground Forces checked in and even delivered the stores to their destinations when necessary, and our Army Air Forces (Air WACs) performed many of the forementioned duties as well as those peculiar to their branch of the service—and the list goes on.

❦

I came into the Service with two primary goals which never abated in intensity. One was to insure the continued freedom for everyone to make their own decisions in the matter of life and liberties, and to contribute to that end, so that the men and women involved could be restored safely and soon to their nearest and dearest. I could not return home until these targets were within reason of my efforts.

Could I save them all? No one person could. I could be thankful that my closest and most beloved were returned alive. I had given my best and hoped never to look at war again.

❦

What alterations had I undergone in the course of three years that made me somebody else—not the girl who enlisted that lifetime ago? Grateful for the varied associations along the way, there were many lessons learned. I now had heightened awareness, emotions well exercised and a heart grown greater—feet grown greater too (remember all those marches?).

Retrospect is that which cannot be put to pen until the passage of time gives it dimension. My restrospection is encompassed in the preceding record of what it was like for me after I was ordered to active duty in 1943 as a soldier in the first permanent female army of the United States!

ADDENDUM

The quantities of print thus accumulated have spilled over into stories published by the Texas Historical Association in their *Southwestern Quarterly*; in the *Nacogdoches Sampler* newspaper of the Nacogdoches, Texas, Chamber of Commerce; *Texas Highways* magazine; the *Long Island Forum*, published by the Friends for Long Island's Heritage of Long Island, New York; and into my *Hey Lady! Uncle Sam Needs You!* tale of basic training, which is available at military historic sites.

BRING BACK THE MEMORIES...

for you, your family, friends, that history buff ...or a long-lost buddy!

Laugh, Cry and Remember takes you back—in the comfort of your home! To order a copy for yourself or to share with a friend, just fill out the form below and mail it in today with your check.

❑ **YES!** I want to bring back the memories!

Name_____

Address_____

City_____State_____

Zip Code_____ Phone _____

Send $12.95 for each book you wish to order. Add $2 for shipping of the first book, 50¢ for each additional book. Allow 4-6 weeks for delivery. Make checks payable to Journeys Press.

Please send me _____ **books at $12.95** ...._____

Shipping ...._____

Tax *(Arizona residents: add 87¢ tax per book)* ...._____

TOTAL amount enclosed ...._____

❑ Please autograph my copy. Address autograph to _____

Send your order and check to:
Journeys Press
P.O. Box 32354
Phoenix AZ 85064-2354

BRING BACK THE MEMORIES...

for you, your family, friends, that history buff ...or a long-lost buddy!

Laugh, Cry and Remember takes you back—in the comfort of your home! To order a copy for yourself or to share with a friend, just fill out the form below and mail it in today with your check.

❏ **YES!** I want to bring back the memories!

Name_____

Address_____

City_____State_____

Zip Code_____ Phone _____

Send $12.95 for each book you wish to order. Add $2 for shipping of the first book, 50¢ for each additional book. Allow 4-6 weeks for delivery. Make checks payable to Journeys Press.

Please send me _____ **books at $12.95** ...._____

Shipping ...._____

Tax *(Arizona residents: add 87¢ tax per book)* ...._____

TOTAL amount enclosed ...._____

❏ Please autograph my copy. Address autograph to _____

Send your order and check to:
Journeys Press
P.O. Box 32354
Phoenix AZ 85064-2354